$\mathcal{P}ra$

'In *Ignite & Write: Th   .ırul Author*, Roxanne has created a well-structured guidebook for any aspiring writer. Drawing from her decades of experience as a ghostwriter, author mentor, and award-winning business owner, she has provided a must-have companion for all those seeking to put pen to paper and publish. With numerous anecdotes highlighting the experience of several published authors, and multiple interactive tasks to prompt and motivate her readers, Roxanne becomes a private mentor for any would-be author along their journey. If you are looking to more clearly understand your 'why', gather the courage and self-belief to write, and adopt a process that will ultimately lead you to publication, *Ignite & Write* is for you.'

 Shari Hall, *author of Perfect Love*

'*Ignite & Write* serves not only as inspiration in life lessons but encourages one also to share them with the almighty power of the pen. Roxanne's vast experience with the written word, integrated with her personality and successes, gift her the rare ability of not writing to the surface of the reader but, instead, to the heart of the reader's creative soul. As a songwriter and author, it's fantastic to see a piece of work with pages so informative created in a fashion that seems to make the words themselves smile. *Ignite & Write* most definitely has the power of connection.'

Wayne Warner, *Nashville recording artist, producer, and author of Backstage Nashville*

'The Mindful Author is a book of encouragement, enlightenment, reasoning, and 'how to' overcome initial fears and objections so that you can get started. When mentoring people in this space, conversations usually

start around fears, concerns, feeling ignorant or apprehensive, seeking guidance, knowing 'how' to start, and solidifying their 'why' to commence writing. This book is the first of its kind to my knowledge and addresses all of this and much, much more. Roxanne's book is a must-read for anyone brave enough to consider sharing their story, as this book will give you all the reasons as to why you should make it happen and take action. The world needs to hear your story, and people want to embrace and immerse themselves in your story. Congratulations, Roxanne, on sharing your stories so that people can gain the confidence and clarity they need to get started!'

Zoë Sparks, author of Strive & Thrive, Healthy & Wealthy, Award & Reward and the SHINE'ing The Spotlight series

'I'm more than happy to put my hand up and say, if it wasn't for Roxanne, my book would probably still be on bits of paper and Word documents all over the place. Working with Roxanne was the thing that brought the book together. And it was her experience of

being able to interrogate me, week on week over three months, that brought the book to life.'

Stew Darling, resilience coach and author of Lead through Life '

'Roxanne's beautiful demeanour expertly inspires and cajoles the best in any novice or experienced author. I love her ethos of embracing the uniqueness of every individual's special journey or story. The world is a better place for the storytelling Roxanne has contributed herself as a writer, and also for the way she has motivated and supported others to share their expertise, adventures, triumphs, and challenges to educate or entertain.'

Joanne Wilson, *author of Renovate Your Relationship*

'As a first-time writer, I was very nervous about taking the next steps after I completed my manuscript. Roxanne was recommended to me by a friend and connecting with her on my book was the best decision I made. She immediately put me at ease and explained to me the process for proceeding with my work. What impressed me the most was her willingness and ability to connect with my book and its characters and understand my motives for writing it. The changes she made to my work clearly demonstrated this. She is highly professional, empathetic, helpful, and insightful. She has given my work the professional touch that it needed. I would unreservedly recommend Roxanne to any aspiring or established writer.'

Alex Gerrick, *CEO of FearLess and author of A Season of Clouds*

'When I started working with Roxanne, I had written a very raw first draft of my book, *House of Shadows*. From the start, she added the fuel I needed to ignite my passion and believe in myself and my message. Her approach was calm and gentle, so I felt supported throughout the process. The day Roxanne presented me a printed version of my manuscript, I was so thrilled that my vision was now a reality.'

 **Janelle Parsons**, *author of House of Shadows*

'Roxanne has a special talent to really bring life to words on paper so much so that I invited her to work with me as my editor for my first book ever – *Stories of HOPE Australia: Everyday People, Extraordinary Stories*. Not only is she an extremely talented writer with many years' experience, but she is also one of the kindest and most patient ladies I have met. She went above and beyond to help me turn my dream of writing a book into reality. I would highly recommend her services to anyone looking to write a book.'

Kerrie Atherton, *founder of Stories of HOPE Australia and author of Stories of HOPE Australia: Everyday People, Extraordinary Stories and Stories of HOPE Australia: Resilient People, Remarkable Stories*

'Roxanne skillfully assisted with the early scripts of my latest book *UnbreakaBULL* and dug deep into my narrative with empathy and beauty to write the perfect synopsis. I highly recommend Roxanne as the perfect partner if intending to write your own story.'

Barry Bull, *music industry icon and author of UnbreakaBULL, A Little Bull Goes a Long Way, My Little Book of Bull, The Bullseye Principle, Take the Bull by the Horns and more*

IGNITE & WRITE

BOOK ONE

The Mindful Author

Roxanne McCarty-O'Kane

Ignite & Write: The Mindful Author
Author – Roxanne McCarty-O'Kane
© Roxanne McCarty-O'Kane 2022

www.roxannewriter.com
hello@roxannewriter.com.au

Facebook: facebook.com/roxannewriter
Instagram: @roxannewriter
LinkedIn: linkedin.com/in/roxannemccartyokane/

ABN: 62660117725

This book is sold with the understanding that the author is not offering specific personal advice to the reader. For professional advice, seek the services of a suitable, qualified practitioner. The author disclaims any responsibility for liability, loss or risk, personal or otherwise, arising as a consequence of the use and application of any of the contents of this book.

The information in this publication is provided for general purposes only. It is not to be relied on as a substitute for legal advice. You should at all times consult with your own lawyer, especially if your writing concerns matters before the court or for any issues regarding possible defamation.

Cover illustration by Cara Ord, www.caraordcreate.com
Editing by Mona de Vestel, www.condorbooks.net, and
Candice Holznagel, @eat.lovetravel
Proofreading, design and publishing support by
www.AuthorSupportServices.com

ISBN: 9781922375186

For Chris, Lilly, and Lincoln.

You have blessed me with the most powerful transformations
of all...

becoming a wife and mother.

Contents

A note from Roxy   1

Transformation through authorship   19

Authentic story   37

Connection   47

    Self   50

    Story   84

    Audience   102

Transformation   127

The pep talk   141

Acknowledgements   149

About Roxy   153

References   157

The *Ignite & Write* series   160

A note from Roxy

Hey there!

I know you have a book inside of you. *You* know you have a book inside of you; this is why we are here. You may have felt a calling for many years to begin to share your life story in the form of a memoir or autobiography or know innately that having a book as a business owner can elevate your credibility to the next level – opening doors to future revenue streams and business opportunities.

Your book calls out to you in the middle of the night, or you daydream about holding your future book in your hands. It has your name on the front, maybe even your photo on the cover, and you cannot hold the excitement and the anticipation of what comes next any longer. Authorship is a life-changing experience, and it will be yours if you stay the course and see your vision through.

I'm not going to sugar-coat this; becoming an author takes a lot of time and effort as well as an investment in money to ensure you have the right team working alongside you to bring your vision to life. But I know that many aspiring authors do not even manage to take the first step. Uncertainty over what to do, when to do it, and how to do it does nothing but hold people back.

But you are different.

You have already taken that first step by buying this book, the second step by opening the cover, and the third step by taking the time to read the content that will provide you with a map for your journey. You are well on your way, so keep up the momentum!

In August 2010, Google conducted a search that showed around 130 million books had been published in human history up until that point.[1] With more than three million books being released by publishing houses and self-published authors in a single year in the United States alone, we are seeing more authors created now than ever before.[2]

While it may seem heartening that so many people are realising their dream of authorship, the reality is that they are the 'one percenters', the people who make the effort to plan and put in the time and commitment to seeing it through. These statistics are not scientific by any stretch of the imagination, but several published articles reflect that as much as 80 per cent of the US population has expressed a desire to write and publish a book at some stage in their lives. When we consider that in 2019, four million books were published and there were 328 million US residents at the time, it was just 1.2 per cent of the population who became authors that year.[3 4]

In Australia, we have a similar outcome. In 2020, more than 22,600 new titles were released when we had a population of almost 25.4 million.[5 6] This meant newly published authors made up just 0.089 per cent of Australians.

With so many people driven by the desire to write books, why is it that only a small percentage of them experience the joy of holding a copy from their first print run in their hands?

Because it's by no means an easy journey.

I have worked with men and women from all walks of life in either a ghostwriting capacity or as a writing mentor, and all of them are passionate about sharing their experiences or knowledge to help others change their lives.

One thing I have learned is this: no matter how intelligent, articulate, or charismatic you are, there is something about the unknown that can be utterly terrifying.

There are so many working parts to releasing a book that it can feel too overwhelming to even start. When your head is filled with *How does it all work? What do I include? How do I publish?* it can all become too much to cope with. It becomes easier just to let the idea remain in your mind or to allow those half-written pages of work to collect dust in your filing cabinet.

There is only one problem with this: your unique perspective and powerful message remains cooped up inside you and not out in the world where it could be changing lives.

So that you know you are in safe hands while going on this journey with me, I'll share some of my story. Like you, for the longest time I didn't think I even *had* a story. It was just my life. There was nothing extraordinary about it or anything that would make people gasp when I would tell it to them. But with the power of hindsight, I now know that every part of my journey was leading me to where I am now.

I was a girl who loved to get lost within the pages of books, in fantastical worlds that whisked me away from the humdrum of life in the small rural town of Wainuiomata in New Zealand. My overactive imagination was the enemy of sleep, and the only remedy was to curl up in the covers with a book and dive into the latest adventure until my eyelids were too heavy to stay open.

This love of words is something I experimented with inside the pages of my childhood diaries, which I kept diligently from the moment I could write legibly until I was a teenager and got too busy to keep recording daily events. Words were my refuge as teenage angst nipped at my heels, but I began to venture away from them after we moved from our sleepy town to the Sunshine Coast in Queensland, Australia.

It was here that my social life took flight. I was the new kid, the novelty with an accent that made saying things like 'fish and chips' and 'six' crack everyone up, and I made some incredible friends at the age of fifteen that I still hold dear to this day.

A visit from the Australian Defence Force recruitment team one day in Year 11 spruiked the benefits of studying at the Australian Defence Force Academy (ADFA). The promise of a challenging environment and the opportunity to travel and to learn incredible new skills, was beyond anything I could comprehend. It was everything my young mind craved. I trained hard, running every day after school, swimming in our backyard pool, and riding my bike everywhere to boost my fitness even more. I boasted an impressive six-pack and had the academic grades that would ensure my selection was straightforward.

However, there was one hurdle that stood in my way. I am an asthmatic. I hadn't been hospitalised since I was a young girl, but a constricted airway often followed a virus even into my teenage years, and in the year 2000, this was something

I had to have cleared by medical professionals before I could proceed with my application.

I was filled with trepidation as I walked into the medical centre with my mum, who had been a pillar of support in my decision to pursue my ADFA dream. *You've got this. Just breathe in and out and don't panic. You will be fine.* I had to fight off the rising tension that gripped at my shoulders. This was the one thing I had no control over. The doctor was pleasant as he asked me to put a mask on and breathe normally. We would start with a standard saline solution, and they would then slowly include an additive that was designed to trigger an asthmatic reaction to see how my airways responded.

I have absolutely no concept of time in that moment of my life. It was as if it were both flying and standing still. I *do* remember the exact moment when I felt my throat begin to constrict and the faintest wheeze escape my mouth. *My body is betraying me!* I was powerless as the wheeze became more prominent and tears stung the corners of my eyes. *It's over!* Everything I had been working towards was ripped away from my hands even as I desperately gripped onto it for dear life.

The doctor's eyes softened as he asked me to remove the mask and take a few doses of Ventolin to return my breathing back to normal. I had no words. I followed instructions as tears spilled silently down my cheeks. He scribbled a few notes down on his notepad and directed me back to the reception area. The moment Mum saw my face, she knew exactly what had transpired inside that small room. I kept myself together as best as I could inside the clinic, but the moment the glass doors closed behind us in the parking lot, I sobbed my heart out as she held me close.

I didn't keep my ADFA goal to myself by any means – it was my plan A-Z and I was so incredibly excited about it. Telling everyone why I could no longer pursue ADFA was painful. It felt like someone was twisting a knife even further into my gut each time I explained the major hurdle I had no hope of being able to jump. On the surface, I was incredibly supportive when my boyfriend and best friend were both accepted to ADFA. Inside, I wanted to scream and throw the most epic tantrum. *I'm being left behind!* As the years passed, they both offered to fly me to base to see what it was like and, of course, to spend time with them, but I declined every time. The thought of having it all right there but beyond my reach was just too much to bear.

For a time, I was lost, and that was not a good place to be when the pressure of the question, 'What are you going to do with your life?' falls off the tip of every tongue as you navigate through those difficult senior school years.

I took some time to grieve the loss of my dream and then started to reassess my options. I liked IT class and could see myself working in the computer industry. Remember this was well before the days of Apps and we were still in the dial-up era, so it didn't seem like a very rewarding career. Ironically, my classmates who did pursue it back then are now probably gazillionaires! I was fascinated by history and considered anthropology or archaeology. I was also hooked on forensics TV shows and thought I could study criminology and forensic sciences – alas my chemistry and maths grades were not up to par so that was discounted rather swiftly. Then I came back to my love of words.

Novelist? Nah! But what about journalist?

I spoke with my English teacher, and she suggested I offer my services at local newspapers to experience the environment. Thus began a year of sporadic free labour, both at the *Buderim Chronicle*, which was just up the hill from my house, and the larger regional newspaper, the *Sunshine Coast Daily*. At the *Chronicle*, I was trusted with writing up small pieces, and I beamed with pride as I held the first edition with my little 5x5 square of copy tucked somewhere between the letters to the editor and the sports pages.

The *Daily* were a little more selective with what I was allowed to do, and my responsibility was largely to input the Pineapple Puzzle solutions. These ran in tiny print and upside down to help those who had trouble solving the activity. Still, I would cut them out and stick them into my folder alongside the column I had managed to acquire in the *Maroochy News* as the publicity officer for the Maroochy Shire Council's Youth Council. It was a voluntary role that opened many doors and provided opportunities to mingle with actual reporters and professional photographers. These relationships would stand me in good stead when it came time to find work as a qualified journalist.

I had found my new passion. Newsprint was clearly in my blood. Interestingly, my first ever job that didn't involve cleaning my dad's bathroom once a fortnight for $5 – where he even completed the dreaded finger-test – was as a newspaper delivery kid in Wainui. Every weekday after school, I'd don my stylish yellow PVC satchel, which was an absolute must in the unpredictable weather, and hop on my bike to meet the delivery bus outside the front of the local BP service station.

I loved delivering the papers, and I became addicted to making a stop at some stage during my round to open the paper and read the coverlines. When coupled with the nightly TV news we always had to watch at home (my kids have no idea how good they've got it with streaming services now), I was well versed in the daily happenings in our corner of the world.

Coming home with ink-stained fingers and smelling like a freshly pressed newspaper was my normal, and I was amused that when I finally did walk into a newsroom as a qualified journalist in 2017, I was transported right back to those sweaty afternoons on my bike and felt pure joy.

Living in a regional town meant journalism opportunities were almost as rare as hens' teeth, so persistence became my friend during my endeavour to land a job. I had been visiting with Andy Kippen, the man in charge of hiring and firing at APN Newspapers at Maroochydore, while studying a dual degree in Journalism and Arts at the University of Queensland. At least once a week I would call into the office on Newspaper Place after a shift at Target at Sunshine Plaza or before an evening shift at Montezuma's in Mooloolaba, which was owned by the incredible Jan Russell at the time.

I would ask Andy if there were any jobs going and it became a running joke because there never were any jobs going. Still, we built up a rapport and I placed myself top of mind for any suitable job opportunities that came up. One day, I did get a call from Andy to offer me an interview for a third-year cadet role at the *Caloundra Weekly* office. At the same time, I was interviewing for a job as a journalist at the local rag in Condobolin, rural New South Wales. Its claim to fame was being the hometown of Australian Idol singer Shannon 'Nollsy' Noll.

Andy's call meant I had a shot at staying on the coast and I seized the opportunity with both hands. Thus began my career as a *Caloundra Weekly* and *Caloundra City News* reporter under the guidance of Candice Holznagel, who is still one of my dearest friends. After Candice moved on, I took over as editor of the two publications and interviewed, wrote, photographed, and assisted the designers for both newspapers. It was a stack of work but I revelled in it. I loved producing something that was appreciated by and connected to the community around me.

I stayed in community newspapers for another six years and wrote for every APN newspaper from Bribie Island up to Noosa as the roving reporter after the big guns realised they could throw me into any office and I would be able to turn out a newspaper by the end of the week. I eventually moved into the *Sunshine Coast Daily* office and stayed there for another four years. In that time, I married the love of my life and became a mother to two beautiful children.

Not long after APN was absorbed by News Limited, I was made redundant. Sure, it came out of nowhere and knocked me for six, but I didn't have much of a chance to experience life as a kept woman. Within two weeks, I was working with Candice once more at the independent magazine *My Weekly Preview* with a team who worked together in a beautiful synergy. It was something other newsrooms had lost in the quest for 'clicks' as news moved increasingly online.

My time at *My Weekly Preview* was magical and I was able to interview some incredible people; so many that I could never list them all here. Some of my most memorable interviews were with Aussie actress Deborah Mailman, singer Guy Sebastian, trainer 'Commando' Steve Willis, comedian Dave Hughes, Sunrise presenter Monique Wright and Dr Chris Brown.

I fangirled hard when I had the opportunity to interview NRL legend Johnathan Thurston and was sweating bullets when I was asked to interview journalist stalwarts Ray Martin and Mike Willesee (probably more so the latter than the former).

After a couple of years at the magazine, I began to think about what was next for me. A career change? More study? Stepping back to focus on being a mum? The answer came after I attended my first ever business conference – the inaugural SHINE Business Women's Conference to be precise. I was able to listen to incredible businessmen and women over three days. This led to me signing a contract to work with a business coach and the seeds were planted for a whole new path forward – ghostwriting.

I was struck by how every single speaker on that stage had written a book, and the more I investigated it, the more I saw there was a market for someone with my skills to help others to get their stories out into the world. It was the perfect fit for a 'fluff girl' like me, who always loved pursuing the human-interest stories in the newsroom.

Ghostwriting is not a profession most people come across every day, and I love that I always get raised eyebrows and a look of disbelief whenever I mention this is what I do for a living. Believe me, it's a much better reaction to the look of concern and suspicion, followed by the slight shuffle away from me, when I told people I was a journalist!

What I absolutely adore about ghostwriting is now my inner fluff girl can spend months on end getting to know each aspiring author, what makes them tick and how *exactly* they came to be where they are when I start working with them. These people have such a passionate 'why' and a desire to make positive change in the world, and to be able to use my skillset to empower them to step up and become the changemakers they want to be is such an honour.

Then there are the go-getters like you, who know you will get so much joy and satisfaction out of writing your book under your own steam. I'm here simply to guide you and offer advice to allow you to follow through with your bold declaration to become an author.

It might seem a bit self-indulgent that I've dedicated this chunk of the book to sharing my story with you, but there is a purpose behind it. Yes, this too is a teachable moment!

I could have simply wrapped it up in a few sentences: 'Hi, I'm Roxy. I'm a non-fiction ghostwriter. I've been a storyteller for fifteen years and I have a growing list of ghostwritten book titles under my belt. I have been able to work with some incredibly driven, passionate, and unique individuals. I've also won some pretty cool awards in the process. I'm going to share my expertise with you now...'

Instead, I have given you insight into who I am as a person and how I found my way into the profession I love so dearly. The reason I've done that is to show you the power of *connection*. Connection is one of the main pillars of creating a book that will resonate with your readers and enable you to make the impact you dream of when becoming an author.

As you may have noticed from the illustrations in this book, I have an affinity with the phoenix. I believe its legend of bursting into flame and being reborn brighter and bolder from the ashes is the perfect symbolism for transformation through authorship. The phoenix represents rebirth, renewal, immortality, healing, and eternal fire. It is also believed that it's impossible to tell a lie in the presence of a phoenix.

I named my interview series *The Phoenix Phenomenon*® because of the transformation that occurs for every person who writes a purposeful book from the heart.

It is an inevitable outcome and one that is often overlooked by aspiring authors when they first set out to write.

By the time you picked up this book, you may have already been 'reborn' by overcoming some sort of challenge or hitting rock bottom. As you write your book, you will rise from those ashes stronger and with more purpose than ever. Alternatively, the process of writing your book is going to be your 'rebirth' and the chance to heal and renew yourself or your business.

Ignite & Write is a trilogy of books that provide you with a step-by-step process to follow that will see you achieve your goal of authorship.

You hold Book One in your hands and this is dedicated to some of the most common hurdles that stop aspiring authors in their tracks. *The Phoenix Phenomenon*® ACT process unfolds in these pages and will remove the overwhelm and uncertainty you have now that you are venturing into the unknown world of writing your book.

You may have experienced one or all of the hurdles at some stage (or all at once!) but know you are not alone. I have combined my knowledge as well as the collective wisdom of authors I have interviewed and worked with over the years to give you the tools you need to clear these hurdles with the athletic prowess of an Olympian and reach that finish line.

Book Two, *The Structured Author*, takes you through the writing process with some useful tips and tricks to help you stay in flow as well as walks you through the process of building a narrative structure. This might seem like a tedious process but, believe me, it is some of the wisest time you will invest in your authorship journey because it will help you to become focused and able to proceed with clarity.

Book Three, *The Published Author*, is dedicated to what comes *after* you have finished that first draft, including how to navigate the many steps of publishing and how to market your book so it reaches your readers.

The steps forward are clear and easy to manage, and you will feel more empowered than ever before to achieve your dream. You will also feel more connected to yourself, your story, and your audience, which will propel you through any future hurdles to becoming the author you've always dreamed of.

I am beyond excited to take you on this journey!

Roxanne McCarty-O'Kane

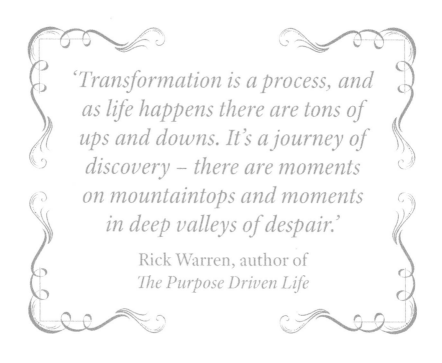

'Transformation is a process, and as life happens there are tons of ups and downs. It's a journey of discovery – there are moments on mountaintops and moments in deep valleys of despair.'

Rick Warren, author of
The Purpose Driven Life

Transformation
through
authorship

‿ 19 ‿

In every second, day, week, month, and year, we are transforming. We are taking in all our experiences, learnings, and interactions and processing them in a way that changes who we are going forward. *If you open your heart up to the process, becoming an author is one of the most powerful journeys you can go on.*

I've lost count of the number of offers I've seen where you can 'become an author' during a weekend retreat or even (I kid you not) in six hours by sending your audio files in for transcription, which is then sandwiched between covers. *Voila!* You are an 'author'.

But there is a very real difference between quickly compiling and releasing a book just to be able to add the title of 'author' to your social media profile and creating something with substance born out of your passion that will serve a greater purpose and resonate with your readers. The crux of that difference comes down to time and your willingness to open yourself up and create a book that is meaningful and authentic for your readers.

In this era when everyone's BS radars are finely tuned, readers can smell insincerity a mile away.

When they crack open the pages, the content will instantly give them an indication of how much heart has been put into its creation. If the answer is 'not much', you will be lucky if they get through the first chapter.

However, we have all read books in our lifetime that have inspired, motivated, and changed us in some way. These are the books that become a part of who we are and have shaped our psyche. When you reflect on what makes these books so special, you will find that connection often lies at the core. The author may have connected with you through their authentic story, the way in which they openly share themselves and their wins as well as their fails, or the way in which they ensure you are at the top of mind as they share experiences or learned knowledge.

There is a universal belief that there is a story in everyone. It is a belief I have held dear throughout my career. Even as a cadet journalist straight out of university, I would get sent out to the small community events, the university open days, and the annual charity fun run, and asked to bring back something noteworthy.

The event itself was never the focus of my attention – it was always the people: the eighty-six-year-old who was competing in the fun run for the sixth consecutive year; the first-year university student with a visual impairment who was studying a traditionally highly visual subject; the first female president of a community Lions Club.

It is the people who make the stories. They provide the most compelling reads where fact is usually stranger, and more exhilarating, than fiction! I was dubbed the 'fluff girl' in the newsroom because I had no interest in chasing police cars or ambulances or sitting in a courtroom all day. It was unusual because they were the most hotly contested rounds.

What I have seen since focusing on ghostwriting and mentoring people to write their own non-fiction books is that there is always a process of transformation that takes place. Being someone who loves nature in all its majesty, I found a great similarity between how a fruit tree grows and how a book is released. So let me indulge you with a little analogy.

Becoming an author is much the same as planting a fruit tree. First, you need the seeds of an idea and the passion to step up and become a changemaker by sharing your knowledge or lived experience with others around you and the wider world.

Once you plant those seeds, you can't just walk away and wait for it to happen – you need to act. Water your idea and nurture it as it grows. Make sure you give it lots of positive attention and sunshine and make it a priority in your life.

You need to be aware that weeds will grow unexpectedly; they come in the form of self-doubt, imposter syndrome, and disbelief that what you have to say is worth being read. These weeds can grow within your own mind or be blown in on the wind in the form of other people's opinions and comments. Like any successful gardener, you need to remove any weeds quickly but gently so you don't damage the already establishing roots.

Be sure that you don't walk away and leave your tree prematurely. Just because a sturdy trunk is now established in the form of a solid chapter structure and many content branches are growing, it doesn't mean that the tree can fend for itself. You will need to continue to give your manuscript time and attention so it grows and evolves into the book you had always envisaged. Failure to do this will leave you with a fruitless tree that never reaches maturity.

When your physical book arrives in your hands, it's like picking that first fruit of the season from your tree. Here, you have something you can offer to the world. Your book could be the life-changing key someone has needed to unlock a better life for themselves and their families.

You were able to achieve this by seeing your seed of an idea all the way through to harvest.

Being the author of a high-quality book is still held in high esteem in professional circles. You then become elevated to expert status and, with some great marketing behind you, the potential to leverage your book to become an industry commentator, a renowned leader, a sought-after consultant, and even a speaker is limitless. You can take it as far as you want.

For those writing for personal reasons, there is potential for a journey of healing, acknowledgement, and empowerment that awaits you when you write your authentic story and step into it fully. You own your mistakes, acknowledge where they have led you in life, and feel the freedom of sharing them so others can make sense of their own world by looking temporarily through your lens. Authors who are sharing traumatic experiences often describe their transformation as a form of healing that has allowed them to feel unburdened by their past.

The key to this transformation is in the foundations – in nurturing those seeds of ideas to create a book that connects as strongly with your core message, values, and beliefs as it does with your readers'. When readers truly resonate with you and your message, they feel like they know you, will like you, and trust the product or service that you offer – the golden trilogy of converting new clients. For those writing their life story, readers who connect with you will be more likely to take your important life lessons on board and learn from them.

You have this book in your hands because you have dreamed of becoming a published author and may have come across some of the common hurdles many aspiring authors face: self-doubt, fear of putting yourself 'out there', worry over who you may offend, perfectionism, and all-around uncertainty over how to proceed and complete the manuscript.

It *can* be a reality if you simply make a start today.

Join the many others who have braved the path on my transformational writing process I have named *The Phoenix Phenomenon*®. Here you can uncover your strongest and most authentic message while weaving your knowledge and lived experiences to create a bespoke, engaging, and inspiring manuscript that can leverage the growth of your business and personal profile.

Your book can unlock new income streams in the form of speaking engagements, hosting workshops, or gaining a larger following through publicity using your author status. This may even lead to you increasing prices for your products or services to match the credibility that comes with being a published author.

The experience of authorship is unique. For some, it is akin to a phoenix, very literally emerging from the ashes to become stronger and more powerful than ever before. For others, it is about strengthening what is already there to move forward with greater purpose and clarity, free of the shackles that once bound them so tightly.

Some authors sit down, free write, and come away with a manuscript. Others spend years picking it up and putting it back down again. *The Phoenix Phenomenon*® ACT method ensures that you have the knowledge and tools you need so you will not fall into the latter category and will be able to move forward with certainty and clarity of purpose. This method of authorship is much more than simply fulfilling a word count requirement and wrapping a cover around it – it is a process that has the potential to transform you, your business, and your life.

An author striving for connection to their readers and propelled forward by a desire to create positive change in an industry or subject will be remembered, celebrated, and supported by those they want to help.

This is where the transformation lies.

There are only three things you need to set off on your journey of authorship:

 An **A**uthentic story.

 A willingness to **C**onnect.

 The openness to **T**ransform.

Every single one of us has a story – I firmly believe that – however, staying true to your **authentic** story and not being worried about what others might think is the first step to transformation through authorship.

A successful author must be willing to **connect** to themselves, their readers, and their vision. If you disconnect from your story and do not fully embrace it, you will create a disconnect with your readers who can see through any hint of inauthenticity. Likewise, without a clear vision of the impact you want to have by sharing your story with the world, you will be disconnected from seeing it through to fruition.

To achieve the ultimate success, you need to be ready to put the effort into all the above to **transform** and reap the financial, emotional, and professional rewards of becoming an author. This is where *The Phoenix Phenomenon*® reaches its conclusion.

What the journey looks like

'I believe luck is preparation meeting opportunity. If you hadn't been prepared when the opportunity came along, you wouldn't have been lucky.'

Oprah Winfrey, media personality,
author, and philanthropist

I created *Ignite & Write* so people who have that spark and desire to write their book can embark on the journey with more passion, purpose, and clarity. For that reason, this is a 'how to write a book' series unlike anything you have read before. While the steps are important, this trilogy focuses on the transformational aspect of authorship and guides you through the journey from a soul-led perspective.

Preparing for the journey means knowing you are ready to give it your all. Considering it takes me on average between three and four months to create a first draft for my ghostwriting clients and this is what I do professionally, you will need to be aware that this process will take time.

Knowing the importance of prioritising your book and committing to regular writing sessions is essential. Without preparing this time, you run the risk of being among the 99 per cent of people who start this journey and never finish. You *can* become a one percenter if you are prepared for what lies ahead.

For first-time authors this realm of the unknown can be daunting, but just know that with this book you will have everything you need to be able to navigate the journey with certainty.

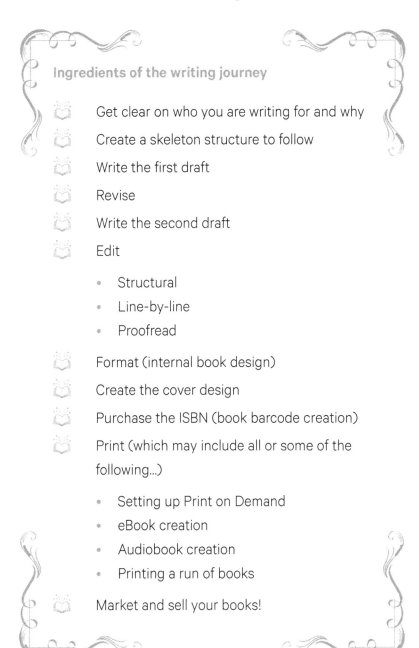

Ingredients of the writing journey

- Get clear on who you are writing for and why
- Create a skeleton structure to follow
- Write the first draft
- Revise
- Write the second draft
- Edit

  - Structural
  - Line-by-line
  - Proofread

- Format (internal book design)
- Create the cover design
- Purchase the ISBN (book barcode creation)
- Print (which may include all or some of the following...)

  - Setting up Print on Demand
  - eBook creation
  - Audiobook creation
  - Printing a run of books

- Market and sell your books!

Remember that it really does take
a team to bring a book to life and
I would recommend not setting
off with the fixed mindset that
you will do it all on your own.

While it can save you some money to self-publish without assistance, it can also leave you open to a world of stress and overwhelm if you are learning to upskill on several different aspects at the same time.

Rest assured there are a myriad of publishers around the world who have teams of professionals that have the expertise to assist you across a range of price points. There is a perfect fit out there for you. But for now, let's take one step at a time.

Am I ready?

*'Everyone thinks of changing the world,
but no one thinks of changing himself.'*

Leo Tolstoy, writer

I have shared my thoughts on how every single one of us has a unique story, perspective, and insight into the world we live in. In essence, we all have a story to tell. But should you take that story and turn it into a book?

It seems an odd question to ask when you have picked up a book that prepares you to embark on the journey of authorship, but it is an important question.

Sometimes, as much as we have the drive and desire to share our message, the timing may not be right. Your experiences may be too raw. If they have only recently been resolved and you cannot recall your past without overwhelming emotional pain, it may be in your best interests to shelve your book idea for a couple of months to heal from your trauma.

I will add a caveat that no authentic writing journey will come without emotion. In fact, the best ones always trigger tears, laughter, and even fear. Being able to tap into those emotions without being overwhelmed is the key. If it is all too fresh, you may gloss over the experiences to save yourself from too much heartache. When this happens, you deprive yourself of the opportunity to heal and you also deprive your readers of experiencing and learning from your authentic story.

If you have not yet accessed professional help to process your trauma, reach out to someone you are comfortable with and begin the process of healing.

> When you can recall your experiences and feel you can write about them openly, you know you are ready to begin your book writing journey.

In many cases a person is ready emotionally and physically. It is simply unfounded fear or self-imposed hesitation holding them back.

I met a highly successful businesswoman – let's call her Steph – who found her business to be booming when the rest of the country was in the first wave of the Covid-19 pandemic in early 2020. Her business grew from being a sole trader to employing fifteen staff with a six-figure turnover within twelve months. Now those stats are impressive by any stretch of the imagination, yet Steph still held reservations about writing her book.

We had been speaking about her book for almost a year, but her main concern was considering whether or not she was writing it too early. 'I feel like I'm still *in* it, like it's all still happening,' she said.

In this case, Steph's business will continue to grow and evolve, but what she already had was her incredible Covid-19 growth story and how she juggled nurturing her newborn son – yes, that was happening too – alongside nurturing her burgeoning business. This would be more than enough to educate, inspire, and motivate other young businesswomen and show them that anything is possible.

Steph could easily make her mark by releasing this book – her first of potentially many – and begin to open the doors she dreamed of that would lead to her becoming an industry expert and a regular on the speaking circuit at corporate events and seminars.

In this case, it was only Steph's mindset that was getting in the way. She felt like she wasn't ready, when really, she had the hard-earned success story and the willingness to share it – the key ingredients to creating a successful book.

If you see similarities in your situation and Steph's, take a moment to look at some of the most prolific authors in any industry. If we choose performance coaches as an example, Tony Robbins has released seven books since his debut *Unlimited Power* in 1987. Brendon Burchard has released five books and a planner since his 2007 release, *Life's Golden Ticket*. Brené Brown has six number-one New York Times bestselling titles under her belt and has been releasing books since *Women & Shame: Reaching out, speaking truths & building connection* in 2004.

The lesson here is that by waiting for the 'perfect time' to release your business book, you may in fact be missing the opportunity to capture your evolution as a person and a leader. Imagine if Robbins, Burchard or Brown decided to wait until 2022 to release their first book? They would have an overwhelming amount of knowledge and experience to share, and they would never be able to cram all of it into one cohesive book.

Once you have determined that you are ready and willing to share your lived experience and knowledge to make your mark on the big wide world, you can move forward with certainty that you are in the right place to make your book a reality.

Call me a dreamer, but I am a firm believer that everything in life is perfectly perfect, even if it doesn't appear so at the outset, and happens when it is meant to. I am often asked by people in business if there is a 'right' time to release a book.

My answer is, 'Whenever you feel called.'

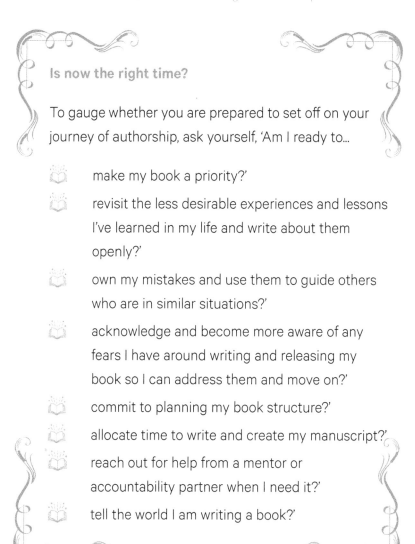

Is now the right time?

To gauge whether you are prepared to set off on your journey of authorship, ask yourself, 'Am I ready to...

- make my book a priority?'
- revisit the less desirable experiences and lessons I've learned in my life and write about them openly?'
- own my mistakes and use them to guide others who are in similar situations?'
- acknowledge and become more aware of any fears I have around writing and releasing my book so I can address them and move on?'
- commit to planning my book structure?'
- allocate time to write and create my manuscript?'
- reach out for help from a mentor or accountability partner when I need it?'
- tell the world I am writing a book?'

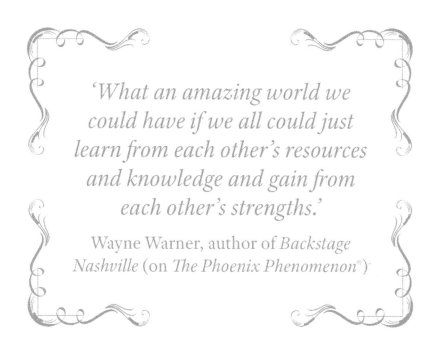

'What an amazing world we could have if we all could just learn from each other's resources and knowledge and gain from each other's strengths.'

Wayne Warner, author of *Backstage Nashville* (on *The Phoenix Phenomenon*®)

Authentic
story

E very single one of us has lived a truly unique life. We may have similar experiences to others, but the way we perceive, process, and incorporate the memories and lessons we take away from these experiences is uniquely ours. This shapes our view of reality and gives us a voice that is one in a billion.

Being brave enough to step up and share this authentic story is a major step towards authorship. There is, however, a step even before *that*. This is where you understand that you have a story to tell. We have a habit of chugging through life on autopilot and we can do this unconsciously for years without stopping to appreciate just how far we have come, what we have achieved, and the impact we have made on the people around us.

When we operate like this, it is hard to see that there is a story inside of us that the world needs to hear. We take our lives for granted and sometimes fail to see the greatness for what it is. I believe in the power of every story that reaches my ears, but it is even more important for *you* to believe in it if you want to succeed.

As you have already taken the step of delving into this book, you have at least an inkling that you have a story worth sharing. If you are still in 'almosting' – that delicious phase where you have felt that spark to begin to write but you haven't quite landed on what that looks like just yet – you will be pleased to know there are several activities in these pages that are designed for you to gain that clarity.

If you are already solid in knowing the power of your story – congratulations! Reading on will allow you to build strong foundations around that story to ease you into the writing journey ahead.

I have spoken with many aspiring authors, and it is easy to gauge quite quickly how at peace they are with their authentic stories.

The people who fully and unashamedly embrace their authentic story will become the most successful authors because they see the value and potential for their lessons to make a tangible difference in the lives of others.

Why do they make the most successful authors? Because people often buy the author over the message. Look at all the health experts in your country. There could be dozens, if not hundreds, who are all promoting a particular diet or lifestyle as the most beneficial, but you will be drawn to a couple over the masses. Why? Because you will connect with their background, their language, their programs, or simply the way they present themselves and their ideas. You will follow and buy from that expert over the rest even though the knowledge they want to share may be very similar.

Those who fall into the middle of the road and only feel comfortable sharing part of their journey may find that their book has weak spots and readers will easily sniff them out. If you are going into incredible detail about one aspect of your personal life or business journey and then pare it right back to gloss over the details on another, your audience will be left scratching their heads.

This is not the place you want to be in because they will start to question the authenticity of your story: *If this part isn't as detailed, they are hiding something. If they are hiding something, maybe they aren't telling the whole truth throughout the book.* The way to overcome this is to solidify the core components of your story. Anything that doesn't add to those components, or work to strengthen them, is better left out.

One of the bravest authors I have had the honour of working with is Janelle Parsons. She had written a very raw, honest, and uncensored memoir that covered her experience with generational abuse.

Unfortunately, many people with these types of stories to tell may think that turning to methods such as writing under a pseudonym or writing their true story under the guise of a fiction novel is the answer – I am as anti-pseudonym as they come and will always ask this question of an author considering fictionalising their story: Do you want to entertain or share some important lessons or knowledge with your readers? I will discuss this further when we go more in depth on connection to story.

Janelle never considered using a pseudonym because she understood the power of her story. From the outset, she was prepared to stand tall and weather any potential backlash from family members she had disengaged from many years ago. She knew that by telling her authentic story without brushing some elements under the rug, she would be able to reach the hearts of people who were experiencing similar abuse to what she endured. She would be able to connect with them, take them by the hand, and show them there is hope on the other side of the trauma. Janelle could help them see that they too could leave an abusive relationship, heal, and go on to live a fulfilling life, just as she had done.

Because of her commitment to authenticity, her book, *House of Shadows,* was making ripple effects even while it was in pre-sale mode in early 2022. It is a testament to how being prepared to stand by your story and own your truth creates the most powerful books.

The fact of the matter is that while there have been some fantastic books that share knowledge through parables, the reader never knows how much of that story is true, embellished, or made up simply to convey an idea. Because of this, they will credit you with being a fantastic writer, but they may not make the visceral connection and be driven to adapt in any way based on the realness of your book.

Authenticity is key and sometimes it can be tempting to opt for the easy way out. To attempt to gloss over defining moments in our life because it's too hard to share them in detail. To pretend that we are truly healed when we are still smarting from the sting of certain experiences. To present ourselves as someone we are not.

I believe there is such a thing as being 'accidentally inauthentic' and this happens when we feel we are not good enough to present ourselves as we are.

Accidental inauthenticity can happen when you adopt a new voice in your writing to try to sound more professional. Your readers will have one version of you through your book that then may not align with the person they find when they connect with you to work together or hear you speak at an event.

Accidental inauthenticity can happen when you bend the truth or fudge the facts to make for a better read or when you feel like your story isn't powerful in its own right and you have to embellish. Throughout this book I cover some of the major self-doubts that creep in for those of you on your path to authorship. Believe me, they are more common than you would ever think, and you are certainly not alone.

One of the major hurdles people who don't usually write have with becoming an author is the word 'writer'. It can feel heavy and carry a lot of weight for people who are doing this for the first time. In my *Ignite & Write* workshops, one of the first things I do is encourage aspiring authors to unburden themselves of that weight. Instead of thinking of yourself as a 'writer', think of yourself as a 'storyteller'. Doesn't the latter feel lighter? More fun? More doable?

All of us can tell a story! What's more, your authentic story comes directly from your heart and your mind. The content is already there; all you have to do is trust that you can tell your story in your own voice.

But what is your authentic voice?

I caution you to be mindful of how you write whenever you sit down at the keyboard. Whose voice is coming through? Is it yours? Or is it the voice of a favourite author you are trying to replicate? Is it the voice of someone you admire and respect? Is it the voice you think your readers want to hear?

Authentic voice exercise

Here is an exercise I do with everyone I mentor to help them to find their authentic voice effortlessly:

 Find a way to record yourself talking. You can use a voice recorder app on your phone, grab a Dictaphone, or simply use the video function on your phone or other device. Have this at the ready.

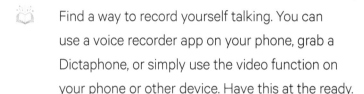 Think of an event that has stirred emotion within you. It can be *any* emotion. It could have made you feel happy, sad, angry, frustrated, shocked, surprised, inspired... whatever it may be. Picture that event in your mind. Play it out. Feel the range of emotions that come with it.

Hit 'record' and tell the story as if you were recalling it for a partner or dear friend who is very close to you.

Don't try to give it any structure; just set your natural storyteller free. Take as long as you need to get through the story; no need to rush it.

When you are finished, listen to it or watch it back.

Pay attention to how you told the story.

What type of natural storyteller are you?

Are you descriptive ... someone who paints a picture of who is where, what they are doing and wearing, and their demeanour before you even start on the events that are unfolding?

Do you go in with a bang and start with the impactful moment and then circle back to build on the context?

Are you very black and white, simply stating the facts and not bothering too much about the details?

Do you have fun with it and present it as if you were telling a joke, building momentum until you drop the 'punch line'?

None of these are right or wrong. Doing this exercise will help you to become aware of your natural storytelling style, the one you employ when you are being your authentic self and don't feel like you must impress anybody.

When you take this view in all your writing, you will have no choice other than to be yourself. Knowing that people who pick up your future book will be innately connected to you, and not some projection of who you think you should be, will help you to cement the fact that you are absolutely, without question, amazing as you are.

You *are* good enough.

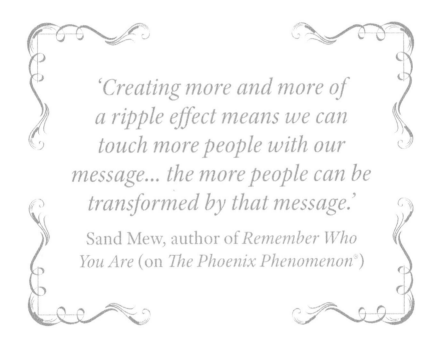

'*Creating more and more of a ripple effect means we can touch more people with our message... the more people can be transformed by that message.*'

Sand Mew, author of *Remember Who You Are* (on *The Phoenix Phenomenon*®)

Connection

Think about the books that have made an impact on your life. They may be across a variety of genres. They may be fiction or non-fiction. It doesn't matter. What if I told you that every single book on your list has something in common, no matter how diverse the subject matter?

Their common ingredient is connection.

You have connected to each of those books in a powerful way. It may be to the author, whom you've come to rely on as a source of wisdom, entertainment, or inspiration. Maybe you are connected to the message within the pages as it has resonated with you on a personal level by connecting to your values. Maybe you have been moved to look at something from a completely different point of view and it has changed or slightly opened you up to new values and beliefs.

When you can incorporate powerful means of connection into your book, you're on your way to bestseller status.

I have genuinely lost count of the number of aspiring authors I have spoken to who have dreamed of writing a book for years and either they haven't made a start or they have written a chapter or two and shelved it. There it sits, gathering metaphorical dust while the person never fulfils their dream of becoming an author.

The key is to create a book that connects as strongly with your core message, values, and beliefs as it does with your readers'.

When you do this, readers can truly resonate with you and your message. They will feel like they know you and this leads to trust.

There can be many different excuses for not moving forward with your book: 'I don't have time', 'I didn't know how to start/ continue', 'No one wants to hear what I have to say...' – on and on it goes. Yet there is still a pull to complete the project, to shift authorship out of the realm of possibility and to make it reality instead.

If this is you, there is one piece of the puzzle missing – connection.

When you are missing connection to yourself, your story, or your audience, you are not in alignment with what this book will do for you. In this section, we will examine how you can become more connected to these three important pillars to ensure the book you create will have impact.

Self

'I've learnt that everybody has stories, everybody has struggle, and everybody has challenges. It's about how we rise from the ashes. How we preserve our own sanity and wellbeing as we're processing those tough times. And then how do we make them have meaning in our life where they make us and help us become a better human being for it.'

Kim Morrison, author of *The Art of Self Love* (on *The Phoenix Phenomenon*®)

Finding your 'why'

Finding your 'why' is so important when it comes to writing a book. I get it... it's a buzz word and one that gets deployed regularly in the personal development world. Buzz words usually exist because there is a universal truth behind them. When it comes to writing a book, the journey is often filled with uncertainty so finding a strong 'why' to anchor into will be worth the effort, believe me.

When you have clarity of purpose, you will be driven to complete your manuscript and see it through publishing so it can be out in the world, serving *its* purpose. Your 'why' will give you the nudge that you need to propel you forward and keep you motivated when it all starts feeling like a bit too much and that little voice pipes up with all those self-doubt mantras designed to stop you in your tracks.

You can think of your 'why' as Wonder Woman's lasso of truth. You can whip it out whenever you notice your mindset beginning to cloud and swing it around until it fills you up with passion, joy, and drive once more.

Having a desire to become an author is a great place to start but drilling down into your motivations for that desire is where you will find your gold.

Without a strong 'why', you are sabotaging your chances of seeing this journey through to the end. Life is so hectic already; it is so easy for your book to slip down the chain of importance and become less of a priority. When this happens, you slip back into the realm of your book simply existing as a dream outcome rather than a tangible creation you are actively working towards.

It's only three little letters, but 'why' is such a powerful question to answer. As the king of 'why' author Simon Sinek says, 'Very few people or companies can clearly articulate *why* they do *what* they do. By *why* I mean your purpose, cause, or belief – *why* does your company exist? *why* do you get out of bed every morning? And *why* should anyone care?'[7]

Whether you are already on the path of authorship or you are still sitting on the fence waiting to take the leap, ask yourself, *Why is writing a book important to me?*

Is it because you want to entertain people? Do you want to inform people? Do you want to share some lived experiences so that they can avoid making the same mistakes? Do you want to share your knowledge to elevate their understanding of a particular subject to another level? Do you want it to become a bestseller? Does your definition of success take money out of the equation, so it rests solely on educating and inspiring?

Is your end goal to become a gamechanger and really make an impact in the world? Or do you want to use it as a pillar for your business to leverage off, opening doors to new opportunities that will take your profile to the next level? Or is it simply about leaving a legacy for your loved ones by documenting your life story so that future generations can understand the life that you've lived?

There are so many different 'whys', and there's no right or wrong. It's about what it means to you and what is going to really light you up as you go through the process. This may sound like a futile exercise but indulge me once more by taking this one step further: ask yourself 'why' four more times. It's called the Five Why Technique.

The Five Why Technique was developed by Sakichi Toyoda for the Toyota Industries Corporation and was used as a tool by engineers to diagnose mechanical faults with their vehicles.[8] As you may know, vehicles are complex systems. Something may appear wrong with your car, but the surface problem may be the physical manifestation of a chain reaction that is being triggered elsewhere in the engine. The Five Why Technique was designed to get technicians to spend more time hashing out what this could be rather than fixing the surface problem and the customer coming back the next day with a different issue because they hadn't reached the core problem.

The technique involves:

   defining the problem

   asking:

- why is it happening?
- why is that?
- why is that?
- why is that?
- why is that?

By the end of this process, the engineers would have a more well-rounded view of the issue and may have reached the root cause of it. It is no surprise that such a reflective inward-thinking tool has been adopted by the personal development industry and it is a powerful means of uncovering your underlying desires and motivations. If we were to apply this technique to writing a book, you will find it really is a magical process to help you to uncover the *real* reason your inspiration to become an author was ignited.

To show you the Five Why Technique in action, I will use my own responses as an example.

   I'm going to write a book.

   Why do I want to write a book?
Because it will help me to reach more aspiring authors and help me to expand my business.

   Why do I need to reach more aspiring authors?
There are so many people out there who want their story to be told and I can only work one-on-one with so many people each year. People might not want to wait or be under time pressures to release their book, however the main thing stopping them is having the guidance to do it.

📖   Why should they not just wait for a ghostwriter? Because the sooner their book is created, the greater the ripple effect and the greater the impact it can have.

📖   Why is this important? Because no one should do life alone and the author's experiences or knowledge could be just the thing someone needs to read or hear at a pivotal moment in their life.

📖   Why is sharing their stories so important? They may have the key to unlocking something within their future readers that will change, or even save, their life.

My 'why' is firmly driven by a desire to help people share their lived experiences and learned knowledge so they can save others the heartache of making the same mistakes and bearing the brunt of the same consequences. My 'why' is about authentic stories, connection, and transformation.

Qualified counsellor Joanne Wilson is known as the 'Relationship Rejuvenator'. She focuses on strengthening and saving relationships to reduce the impact of divorce and separation on the next generation, and she shared her authorship journey as a guest on *The Phoenix Phenomenon*®

series. When asked why she felt compelled to write her book, *Renovate Your Relationship,* Joanne said:

> 'Being in a relationship or being married can be quite an unwanted mirror that reflects any of our selfish or unhelpful behaviours. It is also helpful to remind couples with small children what impact their decisions today will have on them in the future. It is a privilege to collaborate with couples and represent these children I will never meet because they often don't have a voice. They never asked for their parents to be arguing or considering separation, or to be exposed to whatever their traumatic situation may be. I'm here to impact generations on their behalf because the decisions we make today are often replicated by our children. If I can be a part of impacting a generation where, when appropriate, couples learn to hang in there and acquire improved relationship skills that feature the grit of patience, kindness, and respect versus "checking out" when it becomes too tough, then I've served my purpose!'

Take some time to really solidify your 'why'. Once you've completed the five whys, you will have a very clear driver for moving forward. When mentoring writers, I recommend you print out your final 'why' from the Five Why Technique or write it down with coloured pencils or pens and stick it somewhere in eyesight of your primary writing space. That way, when you feel like you are doing the hard yards and it is all becoming too much, you have your 'why' there, right in your face, to remind you why this is all worth it.

Once you've solidified your 'why', you then need to define who your audience is so you can best connect with them to ensure your core messages are reaching them.

When speaking with Sand Mew, author of *Remember Who You Are,* on *The Phoenix Phenomenon®,* she shared her deep experience of finding connection throughout her writing process. It was so profound that I want to share it with you here:

'If you get the feeling that you need to write a book then there is truth to it, you will. Allow yourself the space to really go deep with yourself. If you feel like there is a deep message in you, then give yourself the space to listen closely and deeply. Don't rush it. If it's not quite there yet, then do something to take the brakes off. Clear the layers that are holding you back from fully saying "Yes" to yourself, your message, your value, and your worth that you're sharing with the world because, no doubt, there's so much there. I think that's the biggest part because we can just hold it back. You can wait forever for it, and then it's never going to happen. There are so many people out there who say, "I'll write a book one day." And they never do. I think that's a massive shame. So, it's about saying "Yes", getting clear on your authentic message, and getting yourself help and support to write if you need it... always keep coming back to your own core, your own centre, your own truth. Stand for that, no matter what that is.'

Self-doubt

'There's just so much self-doubt. I had to remind myself that I've got the tools and the skills and I'm passionate about my field. We can really take on board what one person has said, and it can really knock us around when we do. We each have such an amazing unique mosaic brain, so use it. Push past that monster of fear.'

Joanne Wilson, author of *Renovate Your Relationship* (on *The Phoenix Phenomenon*®)

'Who am I to write a book?'

'I don't have anything worthwhile to say.'

'Who will care about my message?'

I'm not joking when I say that I hear this from *every* person I work with at some stage of their writing journey. It really doesn't matter if this is the first time you are writing anything more than a few hundred words or if you have already published several books – self-doubt has the potential to impact every single person.

Self-doubt can creep into every aspect of our lives, so it is only natural the inner critic will pop its head up from time to time to swat away your desire to create, to take a stand, and to stick your neck out for something you are passionate about and truly believe in.

At its core, it's a protection mechanism.

But this is where you need to truly ask yourself, *Why am I being compelled to write a book?*

There is another inner voice within you. One that tells you, *You've got this. You can change lives. You have so much value to share.*

This is the voice of reason, and it is key that you empower this voice to help you through the process.

I had the privilege of speaking with Kim McCosker, the mastermind behind the 4 Ingredients cookbook empire, on *The Phoenix Phenomenon*®. She launched her first book in 2007 and created it simply because we were in an era where celebrity chefs were releasing cookbooks with highly elaborate recipes that required specialist ingredients and techniques to pull off. As a busy mum of three boys, Kim simply didn't have the time for any of that. She craved simplicity.

So, 4 Ingredients was born. The first cookbook quickly became a bestseller, driven by Kim's tireless efforts to market and spread the word far and wide. When I spoke with Kim in 2020, she was about to release her thirty-seventh cookbook and could say one in seven Australian households had one of her cookbooks in their kitchen. An incredible effort to say the least!

But I was surprised to find out that this award-winning author who had built a business empire around her cookbooks was *still* nervous about releasing her latest cookbook a few months after we spoke. It just goes to show that the feelings you experience are not unique, and they can still pop up for seasoned professionals who have been in the industry for many years. Just in case you were wondering, of course Kim's book was a bestseller!

I had the honour of working with an internationally renowned television presenter who had one of the most incredibly heartbreaking childhoods. Despite the unimaginable challenges she faced, she rose to prominence on the small screen and built a life filled with love, success, and passion.

She is the epitome of the heroine in *The Hero's Journey*, someone who overcame all the odds that were stacked against her to triumph. Yet, right up until the release of her book, she felt like her message wasn't strong enough. She was worried that it wouldn't have an impact. She spent countless hours working with hypnotherapists and energy healers, and embarking on personal development courses to strengthen her resolve and belief in herself.

This is where I encourage you to step outside of yourself. Writing a book is a very personal journey but, once the story is written, the messages you want to communicate go way beyond you. This is about your reader. How would their life change if you could show them a way to break free from financial destitution? How would their life change if reading your story empowered them to leave an abusive relationship? How would their life change if they finished reading your book and became more conscious of their health and wellbeing?

> There is no doubt that every book written from the heart will touch the lives of those who immerse themselves in your journey.

This is not about you. In the nicest possible way, you need to get over yourself and get out of your own way. Think about how you can make a difference in the world simply by owning and sharing your story. Imagine receiving feedback from a reader one day that says, 'Your book has changed my life.'

I was invited to attend the book launch of Alex Gerrick's *A Season of Clouds* in early 2022 and I was excited to be able to fly interstate to speak to his 100 guests. I shared how Alex contacted me because he had written a full first draft but was unsure of whether he had a story that people would be interested in.

I called what Alex was experiencing 'almosting'. It's when you almost know that your story is worthwhile sharing with the world. Alex had been driven to write, so he had answered the call that had ignited within him. But when he had completed the first draft, he started venturing into 'almosting'.

Now, it's important to let you know that Alex was the CEO of a non-profit called FearLess, which is an advocacy collective for post-traumatic stress disorder (PTSD). Despite the incredible impact he was having through FearLess, Alex was doubting whether his story, which was inspired by his own struggles with PTSD, would be something people would be interested in.

Through working together, Alex moved well past 'almosting' and on February 17 in the Southern Cross Club in Woden, Canberra, there was not a single shred of uncertainty in him as he addressed his guests. Alex was firmly in gamechanger mode! He had created a book that he was so proud of, one he *knows* will become a resource for people who are suffering. A book that will help people feel like they are not alone. A book that will help readers to feel empowered to seek help and know there is hope on the other side of despair. A book that will save countless people heartache by being able to learn from the lessons that he had to learn the hard way.

A Season of Clouds is Alex's gift to the world. It is his legacy, his way of starting another ripple effect for positive change and of saving lives. Alex knows the power of this book and the massive impact it is about to have on the world. Not only that, but on the night of the launch, he was able to share that he'd given an advance copy to a colleague. Her partner had been struggling with PTSD symptoms but did not want to reach out for help. After his colleague passed Alex's book on to her partner, he was inspired to make that call and had booked in his first session with a counsellor.

Although Alex had set out to make a difference in just one person's life, the fact that he was able to reach that goal before the book was even officially launched gave Alex all the confirmation he needed that his story was worth sharing.

Imagine if that was you on the receiving end of a message like that? How uplifting it would be to know that your bravery has changed or saved a life!

I'm not an expert

> *'We're too focused on "how do I avoid criticism?" and not focused enough on "how do I make a difference?"'*
>
> Seth Godin, author and former dot-com executive

'I'm not an expert! That little voice pipes up for the umpteenth time as you think about starting to write.

I'll let you in on a little secret – neither are millions of other authors! Sure, this may have been the case in the days when traditional publishing houses were king and your only option of making it big in the literary world was to have a certain level of professional credibility and status, or a large fan base that could guarantee your publisher could make some decent coin off investing in your story. They sought out people who were considered experts either through the number of degrees framed on their wall or the social proof that showed people wanted to hear what they had to say.

But we live in much freer times.

The rise of self-publishing and assisted independent publishing has meant the power now lies firmly in the hands of aspiring authors. You no longer must tick all the boxes to get a look in at printing; you can make it happen whenever and however you want to.

Of course, there are pros and cons to the different forms of publishing, which I will cover in *The Published Author*. But essentially, there is no longer a *requirement* for you to be an expert to get your story out there into the world.

I personally would argue that you are the expert on what you've lived and learned. Not only that, but readers, more than ever, are looking for inspiration from people who are just like them. People who have built successful businesses from nothing. People who have stared severe injury or disease in the face and gone on to thrive. People who have overcome unimaginable mental health challenges and now are helping others to navigate their own. The list goes on.

Even those 'traditional' experts are finding they need to tap even more into their personal journeys to provide context and relevance to their readers. Connection is more important now than ever before. Readers may get some satisfaction out of a step-by-step book that shows them how to make one million dollars. However, they will be completely satiated by a book that takes them on the author's journey from poverty to millionaire. They will experience the highs and the lows with them as if they are there. This creates connection: the magic ingredient that will turn readers into supporters and followers and then clients, if this is one of your aims.

I worked with a renowned yoga practitioner, teacher, and leader in one of my first writer mentoring groups. We'll call her Alicia. She is the epitome of a yogi – poised, elegant, and moves with a grace that I have envied since I met her a few years before she joined the group. Every word is carefully considered before she speaks, and I have been able to learn so much from listening to her wisdom. But when Alicia and I began to talk about her vision for her book, she began to detail how she planned to back up all her teachings with scientific research. She had even gone as far as asking one of her friends, who worked in research at a nearby university, if he would assist her with their own trial on mindfulness practices so she could collate data that would be unique to her book.

It might be worth noting that Alicia's background before discovering yoga was in a scientific field. She clearly felt compelled to justify the content she wished to share with 'hard evidence'. However, Alicia's target market wouldn't give two hoots about the science of it all – they just want the techniques and to understand how they work and how they can implement them. I mentioned this to Alicia straight away, but it took her a few weeks to let go of that desire to have everything accounted for. She wanted to be seen as an expert and she had associated this desire with hard facts.

Thankfully, as she began to write, Alicia realised that she was most in flow when she wrote from the heart. She felt stilted and disconnected whenever she ventured into adding in too much of the science behind her concepts. While Alicia could not immediately see that her expert status lay solely in her yoga teachings and how she had been able to utilise them to overcome her own intense challenges, the moment she was able to let go of the expectations of others – writing to please the few who may question her expertise by qualifying it all with facts and figures – Alicia found a sense of ease with her writing. She became an engaged storyteller.

By focusing on what Alicia knew and how she'd come to learn it, she was able to find her authentic voice and share the tools her readers could use to change their lives.

> At the end of the day, I believe that *you* are the expert on yourself and your message.

You are the most highly qualified person to be able to tell your story and share your knowledge. No one can do it exactly like you can.

That's why, when I work with clients in a ghostwriting capacity, they don't just hand me their outline and off I go. It is very much about getting to know their story innately, the words they use, the turns of phrase they engage regularly, and the emotions that charge their communication. In that type of relationship, they are the experts at telling their story and

I am the expert in how to craft their words and intellectual property to engage their readers.

But you have picked up this book because you have a different calling. You know you have the capacity to write your own story with a little guidance along the way.

When I spoke with Joshua Clifton, the author of *The Hospitality Survival Guide,* on an episode of *The Phoenix Phenomenon*®, he shared how he felt the pressure of putting himself forward as an expert when there were so many others in his industry who had been around for much longer than he had...

> 'I constantly felt like I had the weight of the industry on my shoulders and thinking, *Who am I to help assist some of these seasoned vets who've been in the industry for thirty, forty years?* I felt like a bit of a young gun trying to teach the old players tricks. There was a lot of self-doubt that it wasn't good enough and questioning it. There were times when I just wanted to literally throw in the towel, and I was literally tempted to just delete the whole master file completely. And there were just some demons that I just had to fight through; I call them growing pains now because they were leading to something greater. It's very easy to go into your bubble as an author and let self-doubt creep in and you've got to have a good support network around you. I think self-doubt and all that creeps in when your vision is a bit skewed or you're doing

a bit of short-term thinking and analysis, but when you keep that big vision – your legacy, your 'why' – at the forefront all the time, it's normally enough to get you through it.'

The takeaway from Joshua's message is ensuring that you are always firmly focused on your 'why' and the people you can help. There are hundreds of thousands of people, if not millions, around the world who are working in the same industry or sharing a similar story to you. But the way you share it is uniquely yours and there are people out there who need to hear the message from *you*. For those people, you are the expert they have been waiting for.

My mother would be the first to say you can tell someone something a million times, but oftentimes it's when they hear the same message with a different spin that it really lands for them.

I've lost count of the number of times Mum warned me about things as I was growing up and my response was, 'Yeah, yeah I know.' But I did the very thing she warned me against. Then someone else gave me the same message Mum had been spruiking for years and I would immediately take notice, take the message on board, and make the changes in my life. Talk about frustration all round!

It happens on a subconscious level, and we are all guilty of it. My point here is that *you* are that person for some of your readers. While your message may not be 100 per cent unique, the way in which you communicate your message and tell your stories is uniquely yours and there is an audience out there who is waiting to hear it the way you write it.

Don't undervalue the power of your authentic voice in its ability to connect with your ideal reader.

I'm not a good writer

> *'You don't start out writing good stuff. You start out writing crap and thinking it's good stuff, and then gradually you get better at it. That's why I say one of the most valuable traits is persistence.'*
>
> Octavia E. Butler, author

How many times have you said 'I'm not a good writer' out loud or thought it in your head when someone has told you that your story is so powerful that you should write a book?

I challenge you to look beyond whether you are a 'good writer' or not. Whose measure are you using anyway? If you've done the deep dive and worked on the authentic voice exercise in the previous chapter, you may be starting to realise that what you have to say really is worthwhile. I'll tell you right now that the technical side of writing can be worked on once you have completed your first draft.

I've touched on it already, but if this mindset block is hounding you, it's time for a mindset flip! Instead of calling yourself a writer, step into your role as a storyteller. It's an innate ability that we have as humans and a skill we have been honing since the beginning of communication. Cave drawings, cautionary fables, songs, films, books... all of them are forms of storytelling. While cave drawings were a means for one generation to communicate where to get the best berries and where a known jaguar patrolled the bush, the modern equivalent – books – are every bit as powerful in educating and inspiring. I'll bet the cavepeople who toiled away on those drawings didn't question their ability to tell their story and neither should you.

It's true there are some barriers to written communication that can mean it takes a lot longer to write your book. I have worked in a ghostwriting capacity for several people who have dyslexia and some for whom English is a second language and having someone to do the heavy lifting for you when it comes to writing may be your best option in these types of cases.

Most of the time, you already have the skills to be able to get your message across, it's usually a matter of getting out of your own head and letting the words flow through you. We can get caught up in the 'how to', perfectionism, and doing it right. The fact of the matter is that there is a whole world of professional editors out there who can polish up even the roughest diamonds of content. Every manuscript, no matter what the state of the first draft, will go through several rounds of editing as a matter of process. The key ingredient is the content you create. They need to have something to work with!

I met with a farmer whom I will call James in late 2018. He told me he had written his life story and he wanted me to look over it. James had lived a hard life, growing up in Sweden during World War II and emigrating to Australia as a young lad with little to no English skills in the 1960s. He built a life for himself here and wanted to share the incredible things that had happened to him along the way.

A two-finger typist, James laboured away at the keyboard for countless hours over several years, and he proudly handed me a USB stick that contained his precious memories. I opened the file with great anticipation when I got home, excited to get to know James and his incredible stories, which he had given me just a taste of during our meeting.

My breath caught in my throat when I opened the document. There was absolutely no semblance of grammar or punctuation. At. All. The first thing I noticed was there was not a single space between sentences in his writing. Full stops were followed immediately by the first word of the next sentence. Names and places were never capitalised and there wasn't a single quotation mark or comma to be found anywhere.

I wondered, *What the heck have I signed up for here?* And believe me, I have never been so grateful for Microsoft Word's Find and Replace feature (this may become your best friend!) With sentence spacing introduced, I set to work on the rest of his story.

The presentation was horrendous, there is no doubt about that. Many would question at that stage if he was worth the effort, but the truth is, once I let go of my grammar perfectionist and just settled into the flow of his story, his content was gold! I laughed, I cried, I even became infuriated at one stage due to the inhumanity of one of his experiences. On the surface, James was not a 'good writer' by any stretch of the imagination! But when I began to polish up what was there, he was an extraordinary storyteller.

He was able to articulate his life experiences in a way that was uniquely James. He did not try to be poetic with his descriptions or fluff around topics. As a man of the land, he was blunt and to the point. It is what people who know him would expect and he was happy to deliver something that was authentic. When he was done, he knew he could call upon someone like me to help him get his manuscript to the point where it could be published. He was ready to fulfil his long-held dream of being an author. You'll be pleased to know that James released his book in early 2022 and couldn't stop smiling like a Cheshire cat!

> Just remember, all you
> must be is yourself.

You do not have to sound like a learned academic or be able to weave in pop culture anecdotes and jokes with ease. If this is your natural way of being, embrace it! If it's not, leave that style of writing to someone else. Readers connect with the author first before they deem their message worth listening to, so it is vital that you are authentic in the way you write.

Come back to your 'why', which is hopefully on your wall by now! Knowing what you are working towards and why it is so important to you will often give you the motivation to keep going. Once your mindset is rock solid after you finish this book, you can work with a writing mentor to help you whenever you find your momentum slipping away or you simply aren't sure what direction to go in next.

As I will cover in *The Structured Author*, having a strong skeleton structure in place before you begin writing will help you to stay on track and not write yourself into a corner. If you need help with this step, you can join the growing number of people who have graduated from my *Ignite & Write* workshop days with a bespoke structure in hand, ready to flesh it out with their stories.

If the idea of sitting down and writing tens of thousands of words over time does induce sweats or anxiety, there are ghostwriters like myself who have the skills and the know-how to be able to craft your book for you in your own words without much of a time commitment on your part at all. In fact, you would never have to touch a keyboard!

I spoke with Leon Stensholm, the author of *It's How You Think,* on *The Phoenix Phenomenon*®, and he shared how he never let his perceived lack of writing ability hold him back from writing not one but two books *and* releasing a journal.

> 'I was actually a super quiet, shy kid and my academic levels of skill were very poor. My writing skills were very, very subpar, even up until my heyday months ago. I never really put too many sentences together. And it's funny how just through a new idea to write a book all of that changed. I was getting some coaching at the time and when they suggested that I'm like, "Dude, I don't even speak that well. I can't even write a letter, let alone write a book." And he goes, "Leon, you have a crazy story." And I thought about it for a second, and I'm like, *Well, actually, yeah, it is a crazy story.* I thought about it for another fifty-nine seconds and I rang him back and said, "I'm going to do this thing." I just went straight home and started writing. I don't know where all this stuff came from.'

Knowing that your story has worth and trusting in your ability to tell your story without questioning your ability is going to help you to get past the fear of not feeling up to par as a writer. Remember, your job is to communicate your story. Others can polish up your diamond so it is publish-worthy and help you to take it to the next level once you have created the initial content.

I don't know how to start/continue/finish

*'Writing is an act of faith, not
a trick of grammar.'*

E.B. White, author of *Charlotte's Web* and *Stuart Little*

This hurdle is closely linked to perfectionism, and it can stifle even the biggest flame of inspiration if you let it. As the Chinese proverb says, 'A journey of a thousand miles begins with a single step.' Here's the kicker – many aspiring authors are so worried about starting at the 'right place' that they don't start at all. The fact of the matter is you will never reach 10,000, 30,000 or 70,000 words if you never write a single one.

We can get so caught up on 'doing it right' that we are paralysed when we don't know the 'right' way forward. Throughout my career as a journalist, I have been able to interview many great Australian authors, including Liane Moriarty, Di Morrissey, Judy Nunn, Mark Brandi, Rhiannon Wilde, and Andy Griffiths.

I always ask what their writing process looks like, and I have learned a very valuable lesson – there is no 'right' way to write a book.

Some authors will sit down with a loose structure and free write, allowing themselves to channel the words, never really knowing where the journey will take them. Others take a more strategic approach, planning a strong structure and then writing within those parameters. Note that both successful outcomes involve *structure* to bring purpose to the time you invest in writing.

When I interviewed country music star Wayne Warner about his book *Backstage Nashville,* he shared how he sat down at the computer and wrote his entire manuscript in one go.

> 'First of all, you have to know you have one [a message]. And second, you must write that first sentence. Know that you have a story and obviously tap into a mentor who can encourage you and to help you to tell it, and know that someone is going to learn from you and that you could encourage so many people from your story. I mean, for everything that's ever happened to you, all those times that you sat alone, crying when no one else was looking, or worrying, or celebrating, you were with you through it all. You've got an amazing story to tell and, I guarantee you, it's as amazing as you think it is. So, tell it. Let us learn from some of the things that you've been through. Some of us probably are going to have some

challenges like that and you might be able to help us get through it. Let us laugh at some of the things you laughed at. Some of the jokes we'll never get to hear otherwise. Some of the funny things we'll never get to do which you did. Is it going to be scary? Yeah, but it's a fun kind of scary and it's very rewarding. That's my advice from a little country singer in Vermont.'

He didn't worry about doing it 'right' and he certainly didn't get stuck on the 'how to'. He felt a calling in his heart and he followed it.

I teach writers to walk the line between structure and inspired writing.

Structure is important because it keeps you focused and helps you avoid writing yourself into a corner – this is where the dreaded writer's block lies! However, I don't believe sticking to the structure at all costs is the answer. Once you begin the journey to authorship, your mind will offer up so many incredibly delicious ideas, unearth relevant memories, and remind you of the golden nuggets of information you have learned over the years. They may not be there at the outset while you are planning, but they drop in as you begin to delve deeper into your writing. Having the flexibility to capture these insights and include them in your book is the key to creating something that is equal parts structured *and* moving, connecting in a way that is unique to you.

The Structured Author has a step-by-step process to structure your book. In the meantime, stop blocking your own creativity with worry about being 'right'. I can confidently say that when it comes to the number of people who have become authors when they initially had no idea how to start, the figure would literally be in the millions. You don't have to reinvent the wheel; just find someone who has done it before and learn from them. Enlist the help of a mentor who can help you with planning out your structure and holding you accountable to achieving your goals. A great mentor will also help you through any emotional blocks you have throughout your journey and offer you advice and strategies to help you overcome any hurdles you come across on your way. I know a good one – her website is at the back of this book. 😌

I don't have enough time

> *'The key is not to prioritise what's on your schedule, but to schedule your priorities.'*
>
> Stephen Covey, author, businessman, and keynote speaker

I get it, everyone is time poor. Everyone from business owners, parents, and employees to retirees can feel like there are not enough hours in the day. But what if I told you that was just a state of mind?

It happens to the best of us. You set out with good intentions and writing is a priority for a week or two, but then it starts to slip down the list. Your work, partner, kids, Netflix... everything seems to demand your time and you forget about the passion that once burned for you to write the book that calls out whenever you have a moment to breathe. This could go on for weeks, months, and even years. I have worked with people who have let this dream languish for decades! There is nothing more painful than delaying the realisation of a dream. When that dream of releasing your book could enrich the lives of others as well, it is a tragedy that it is not seen as vital to achieve.

I had the honour of working with Eufrasia Gagliardo in 2021. She is a successful businesswoman, mother, and grandmother and has dedicated her life to all three in equal measure. Eufrasia had a long-held dream of writing a book but had been so selfless in her support of her husband, children, and then grandchildren that there was little room for her to dedicate the time to her book.

More than two decades passed after her initial ignition – that spark of inspiration that calls us to write – before she contacted me. During those twenty years, she had written out the rough draft of a series of short stories she wanted to compile into a book. Written in Italian, they captured the incredible people she had met and learned valuable lessons from during her younger years living on the island of Massawa.

We were able to work together and, in just a few short months, translated those notes into English and added half a dozen more stories to her growing collection as more memories from her past came to her in the middle of the night. I'll never forget the pure rush of emotion from both of us when I handed Eufrasia the first draft of her book. This was magnified tenfold on the day when she launched *Living on the Pearl of the Red Sea: The unique people of Massawa.*

This unbridled joy and sense of achievement is something I wish every aspiring author would feel, yet so many don't.

The perceived constraint of time is often the biggest reason why people don't achieve their goal of authorship.

I always manage to find time to binge on a few episodes on Netflix. Or to mindlessly scroll through Facebook or Instagram. *I'll just quickly check what's happening,* I tell myself as I open the app, but once the updates on my nearest and dearest are complete, I am suddenly watching inspiring videos and clicking through to gossip websites and all manner of other things. Talk about an epic waste of time!

It's important to remember that many successful authors are business owners or fulltime workers, raising children, participating in various volunteer organisations, and attending multiple after-school and weekend sports, and they *still* manage to find the time to write. They are the successful authors, the ones who seize the bull by the proverbial horns and run with it.

Kym Cousins, whose book *Selling with Heart* has become a multi-award-winning business title and an Amazon bestseller, shared on *The Phoenix Phenomenon*® how she grappled with time management and making her book a priority when she began writing her manuscript.

> 'When I started writing, it flowed freely. So, I wrote, and I wrote, and I wrote, and I wrote, and I wrote, and then I got tired, and I stopped, parked it, and got busy with different priorities and it was hard to get started again. The best advice I had from my mentor was to write something every day. I didn't necessarily follow that advice. Of course, I now wished I did. Some of the things that came up for me was thinking, *What am I doing? I'm not an expert. No, no one's going to read this. I'm being indulgent. No, there's no market for this. Why would I bother, no one's going to buy my book.* Oh my God! All that self-doubt came up several times and I had to slap myself down and keep going. And I remember having a couple of discussions with you, Roxy, and you said, "No, no, it's okay.

Keep going." My mentor was saying the same. The more they said that to me, the more I said, "You just watch me.""

We all have the same twenty-four hours in every day, but how you spend your time will dictate whether you achieve your book dream or not.

Schedule a regular window of time that you dedicate solely to writing. There is no universal 'best time' to write. In fact, it is very individual, and this can be a great time to start to take notice of when you are very goal-orientated and focused during the day, and when you tend to start to daydream. Believe it or not, the latter is the best time to write!

Cognitive neuroscientist and Berkeley lecturer Dr Sahar Yousef suggests when productivity dips, creativity soars and people who consider themselves early birds are at their most creative late morning.[9] In contrast, those who are night owls are the most creative in the morning when they are yet to fully wake up.

If you are serious about making this dream of yours a reality, you will find the time. You will make time in your schedule with ease because you have clarity over what your book can do for you, your business, and your readers, ensuring any temptation for your book to fade away for another decade is dead in the water.

This is what weeds out the 'one day' authors to the dedicated ones. You will be launching your book to the world while they are still staring at a half-completed first chapter on their computer screen.

Story

'Your story and the challenges that you're going to tell in your book are the stepping-off point for someone else. That someone else doesn't have to go through all the same pitfalls and mistakes that you've made in life because you are the stepping stone that gets them on to greatness. So, treat it as a service to fellow human beings. You've got a responsibility to tell your story. The world needs more normal people to tell their stories.'

Stew Darling, author of *Lead through Life*
(on *The Phoenix Phenomenon*®)

Once you feel connected to yourself and know you have the power to write your book and make an impact in the world, the next step is ensuring you are wholly connected to your story.

We've talked about the importance of having an authentic story and it is fair to say we all have one, but how you communicate it on the pages of your book will be the deciding factor on whether your book fulfils your 'why'.

Authenticity is paramount when you want to convert readers into clients or to encourage readers to make real and lasting changes to save their lives or simply just to learn from your wisdom so they do not follow the same destructive path you may have been down.

I'm not going to lie, it is a scary process laying it all on the line as you write, especially when you are sharing parts of your life that you would often leave under lock and key.

It takes an enormous amount of bravery to write a memoir or autobiography or allow your business book to venture into personal territory – but it is essential.

The allure of writing under a pseudonym, glossing over the more gut-wrenching chunks of your book or even leaving them out altogether can become all too attractive. But I urge you to stay the course and to stay true to your original intention for becoming an author.

I will add a little disclaimer here. While I am all for people seizing the day and following inspiration when they are called to write, it's important to consider if now is the right time for you to be doing this if your story is based around a traumatic experience. Ask yourself, *Am I ready? Can I talk about this incident without being re-traumatised by it?*

It is true that the most powerful books are the ones where the author can dig deep and share freely about their emotional state and physical sensations, and be as descriptive as possible about their thoughts and feelings at the time. If your story is still unfolding or you are still recovering from the blows, I encourage you to seek support and give yourself time and space to heal. If you want to see progress on your future book, perhaps start keeping a diary or create a digital file to which you can add notes as they land in your mind, but looking after yourself is more important than pushing through with a full manuscript writing process to the detriment of your mental health.

Remember, it is when you are stronger and more at peace with sharing your story that you will have the most impact.

Kerrie Atherton featured small snippets of her life story as the first chapter in both of her *Stories of HOPE Australia* books, covering several topics from sexual abuse as a child to substance abuse and alcoholism as well as dealing with grief. All of it was heavy content, but Kerrie had given herself the time to heal before she stepped up and became an advocate and professional support for people who were walking the same path as she did many years beforehand. On *The Phoenix Phenomenon®*, Kerrie shared how she was able to break through her triggers to be open in her books:

'That has been a real process. I think with the incident that happened with me when I was sexually assaulted by a paedophile at nine, I've really dealt with that. The rape when I was seventeen was the thing I found the most difficult to write down and process because I didn't start to emotionally heal from that until about four-and-a-half years ago. So that would be why I kept getting stuck on that. But being a counsellor myself, and undergoing a lot of professional supervision as well as talking to other people about the things that I've gone through, I have been able to heal. It's a very slow process to be able to recover from these things. I don't think it's until we fully recover that we're in a space where we're able to be that raw and vulnerable. From that point on, we can truly help others because we're speaking from a point of recovery where we can give hope, not from the state of still being in that victim mentality.'

No matter what the subject matter of your book may be, feeling fully connected to what you are creating is the key to success. Readers have well-honed bullshit radars these days and will be able to tell if the person you present yourself as within the book is very different to who you are as a person in real life. This will only serve to create a chasm between you and your reader, which is the exact opposite of the outcome you want. Take a few deep breaths, step into your story, and begin to tell it.

The slippery slope of pseudonyms and fictionalisation

'Chance is perhaps the pseudonym of God when He did not want to sign.'

Anatole France, journalist and novelist

I have lost count of the number of times I have spoken to an aspiring author who has shared the most incredibly powerful story with me over the phone or in person and I get goosebumps as their emotional language paints a vivid picture of the struggles they were faced with and how they found the power to overcome them.

Then, they come out with something like this, 'I'm going to write it as a fictional story with characters based on people who I don't want to identify.' Or 'I think I'll write this under another name so people who know me won't think any less of me.'

It is noble that their wish to protect those around them is at the forefront of their mind and I know how hard it is to share something that is dear to your heart knowing it has the potential to hurt someone you love. The truth of the matter is that both of these actions dilute the power of what you want to share.

By writing under a fictional name, you instantly create a disconnect between yourself and your reader. By turning your poignant reality into a novel, you are presenting your authentic story in the guise of entertainment – it simply won't be taken seriously.

Learning to see the value in her story was a journey for Leigh Robshaw while writing her memoir *You Had Me at Hola*. She shared on *The Phoenix Phenomenon*® how her self-doubt stopped her in her tracks for two decades before she was able to realise how her story could help people around the world.

> 'I didn't really think, *Oh my God, my life would make an amazing book*. I thought, *I have to get this story out*. It was like a little creature inside me that would not shut up and I had to get it out, but I was terrified of writing a memoir, writing a true story, and I really avoided it for twenty years. I just kept pushing it down, thinking, *No way am I going to tell this story*, because I was worried what people would think of me. I thought, *I'll do it as fiction*. I tried to write it as fiction quite a few times and in a few different ways and it just never felt authentic. I just felt like I was trying to force it to be something that it wasn't. It felt to me like it's a true story and you have to just get over

yourself and write it as authentically as you can and try not to worry what people think of you.'

Whenever I get goosebumps hearing someone's story for the first time, I strongly encourage them to consider maintaining the authenticity of their book by stepping into it and owning the reality of their life.

Only then will the storyteller be able to truly connect with their reader and impart the wisdom they have been compelled to share.

The dangers of using a pseudonym

Consider the three main reasons why you risk destroying the credibility of your book by fictionalising it:

If you want people to adopt the strategies you want to teach, they first need to connect with the author or the character, and the latter can be difficult to achieve.

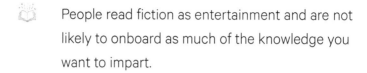

- People read fiction as entertainment and are not likely to onboard as much of the knowledge you want to impart.

- Even if you market the book as being 'based on a true story', the reader will never truly know which elements are real or the work of your imagination. As they say, fact is often stranger than fiction, however the impact will be lost as the reader may likely assume the more outlandish events have been woven in for effect. This greatly dilutes the potency of your story.

In terms of pseudonyms, you may have heard of Mary Westmacott, Robert Galbraith, and Richard Bachman, but it's much more likely you've heard of their real identities – Agatha Christie, J. K. Rowling, and Stephen King.[10] Even famous authors have resorted to pseudonyms in order to branch out into new and unexpected genres without alienating their loyal fans or, in King's case, to have more stories published without oversaturating the market under his own name.

However, these literary powerhouses have huge marketing machines behind them that can help them get their books onto shelves while maintaining that veil of anonymity – for a time anyway. First-time authors and most self-published authors simply don't have that luxury.

In my belief, using a pseudonym for a non-fiction book is a big no-no. To me, it removes a vital connection point with your reader and can become a logistical nightmare when it comes to marketing and selling your book. You would have to outsource all of this to a third party to maintain your distance from the book.

If you feel that you still need to hide behind another identity to release your book, it may be time to rethink if you are ready to take that step.

Half-truths

> *'Half a truth is often a great lie.'*
>
> Benjamin Franklin, writer, scientist, inventor, statesman, diplomat, printer, publisher, and political philosopher

While hiding behind fictional characters and storylines is an extreme way of obscuring your authentic story, another is to only paint part of the picture for your readers. It's like you are giving them a glimpse behind the curtain but they are not allowed to step right through and join you.

I'd like to share a story of an aspiring author I will call Leah, whom I worked with in 2019. Leah had already completed her manuscript and wanted my feedback on what she had created before she proceeded to publishing. She was driven to share her story – it had been calling her for several years – but she was incredibly nervous about the repercussions from her immediate family by opening up. I read her manuscript with great anticipation and made notes throughout on areas where things started to get a bit vague or I got the feeling I wasn't getting the full picture. When I came back to Leah with my notes, her eyes widened and she began somewhat of a confessional.

It turned out that *every time* I felt a disconnect with the story, she had withheld something vital. Something that would help readers understand why things were unfolding the way they were. Each time, she had chosen to gloss over something to protect herself from retribution from her family. She was convinced they would read her book and sue her for defamation.

It sounds like a noble thing to do but, in the process, she had made herself sound like the cause of all her life's problems. The reader would deduce that she was to blame for the emotional and physical abuse she endured and she was incapable of making a solid decision. Knowing her professionally, I knew this was far from the truth, and in her bid to protect others, she had made herself sound like a 'clueless airhead'. Her words, not mine!

In trying to protect herself from her parents, the authenticity of the story had been lost. I knew how important it was for Leah not to aggravate already strained relationships within her family unit, so I presented her with this solution: write about the events from your perspective. How did this situation make you feel? What was the impact it had on you? How did it change your outlook of the world? What are your memories around this?

The fact is, when you write solely from your perspective and present your thoughts and feelings without putting meaning behind someone else's actions or words into their mouths, you are simply presenting your world view to your readers. No one can tell you that it's wrong. It's authentically yours. They can take issue with what you want to share, sure, but they can never argue that you are wrong.

I was delighted when Leah took this advice on with gusto and re-wrote the manuscript, adding more background and detail to her story. Of course, there were some elements that we chose to leave out because they simply weren't relevant to the overall themes and messages. But the transformation was incredible.

Leah's book became one that embraced her challenging journey through life while adequately showing the hurdles she had to overcome to achieve the level of success she had. Even more, it highlighted how she became stronger as a woman with each challenge – showcasing the true hero's journey for what it truly was.

I'm not saying all her fears disappeared entirely, because they didn't. Right up until the day Leah released the book, the worry remained. However, helping at least one young woman to know how strong she is and understand she can overcome anything that is placed in her way, became more of a focus and a driver for Leah.

I am pleased to say Leah released her book to great fanfare, having amassed an impressive online following with her authenticity while she was creating her book. When people realised her realness and rawness was also carried over into the pages of her book, it was an instant hit. She sold her first print run of 2000 books without batting an eyelid!

Leah is a prime example of how marketing from the early stages of writing your book will pay great dividends by the time you are due to release it. I cover more on this in *The Published Author*.

There are absolutely some cases where you must creatively navigate what you share within the pages of your book.

Stories that deal with domestic violence, government, or military agencies mean that some identities and key details will need to be changed and/or omitted.

Rest assured this will not compromise your authentic story and a simple disclaimer or explanation on your imprint page will advise your readers some names and identifying characteristics may have been changed to protect people. I share some tips on name-changing in *The Structured Author* and also discuss defamation later in this book.

Messing with timelines

> *'After nourishment, shelter and companionship, stories are the thing we need most in the world.'*
>
> Philip Pullman, fantasy novelist

I get full-body goosebumps when I hear the kind of story that you know could possibly be adapted for television, Netflix, or even the big screen. There are so many people walking around with larger-than-life stories to share. You know the ones! They make you question why real life is often so much more unexpected than anything even the best fiction writers could dream up.

I worked with a client in 2018 who had lived the most incredible life. Let's call her Shelly. She was a public personality and she had kept her personal life shielded from the world. Shelly was preparing to lay it all out there, and boy, was it juicy. Shelly's story dipped into the world of sex and drugs on an international scale, also touching on domestic violence and international crime syndicates. Like I said, stuff you couldn't even make up let alone imagine all happened to a single person.

Shelly had grand plans for her story. When we first met, she declared that she was working towards having her book not only make international bestseller, but it would feature on Oprah's Book Club and become a blockbuster movie in the future. Her energy around this was palpable and made working on this project so uplifting.

But I want to alert you to the potential to fall into a trap when you go into writing a book with the aim of it becoming a film or streaming series – the temptation is there to alter timelines in a bid to make the story even more sensational. While we were working together, it was suggested by Shelly's husband that perhaps we could combine events or slightly shift the order they happened. I had to put my foot firmly down on making any of these changes.

'What's the harm?' you might ask.

Authenticity.

If you are presenting your book as a memoir or an autobiography, authenticity is king. If you are releasing your book as a pillar of your business or to elevate your profile and open doors for you personally, authenticity is king. If you are writing your book simply to share your lived experience so others can learn from your mistakes, authenticity is king.

While replacing a name here or there is perfectly acceptable to protect identities, changing, adapting, twisting, or manipulating any of the factual events or timelines is a big no-no because it compromises the authenticity of the book. This is a direct reflection on *you* as the author.

If readers must question the validity of something they have been presented as fact, they will lose their trust in you and everything you have set out to achieve will be for nought.

This is particularly poignant when elements of your story are linked to historical events, like 9/11 or a World War, or are in the public record, such as court documents or news articles that can easily be searched on the internet. Shelly's story had elements that were 'Googleable'.

Your job as the author is to capture your story in the most real, raw, and authentic way you can. It is up to the docuseries directors or Hollywood producers to put their spin on it once they've paid you the big bucks for the rights to adapt your book! Every time you watch something that is based on a book of any kind, you will see a disclaimer somewhere that the creators of the production have injected their own creative licence. It will read something like, 'Based on a true story.' Scriptwriters and producers are the ones who can choose to mess with the order of events to create a more intense dramatic effect and audiences expect that will likely happen.

Believe that your story is powerful enough without the Hollywood lens! By staying truly connected to your story and telling it authentically, you will still be able to draw the attention of screenwriters and producers as your authentic self.

Backing yourself

> *'Believe in yourself. You are braver than you think, more talented than you know, and capable of more than you imagine.'*
>
> Roy T. Bennett, author of *The Light in the Heart*

If you type 'How to write a book' into Amazon's book title search you will find there are more than 10,000 options to choose from. Have a go at 'Meditation' and there are more than 100,000! Unless you have stumbled across an absolute niche that is yet to blow up, the chances are this will be the case for just about any subject matter you could possibly write about.

For some, this could be enough to quash any motivation to write their own book. It's all been done before, right?

Wrong!

Unless you venture into pure plagiarism – which is highly frowned upon and will be a costly exercise for you – your book will be unique no matter what the subject matter. Why? Because it comes from you. It is written from your perspective and incorporates your lived experience and your knowledge. While some of the ideas may not be original, they are shared through your viewpoint (appropriately referenced of course).

Remember my long-suffering mum? You can hear something a million times, but when it is presented a certain way by the right person, the message finally lands. Remember the time when you read something and had that real a-ha moment? When a single line from a book you've read changed your life? You could be that person for someone else.

There is no bigger thrill than speaking with an aspiring author who has an innate knowing that they must put it all on the line. They understand the power of authenticity and how it can create the most poignant connection to their readers – the people they want to inspire.

Often it is the people who have lived the most extraordinarily challenging lives who are the most unashamedly at peace with their authentic story.

They know it has not always been sunshine and rainbows, and they have perhaps made some poor decisions that have resulted in less-than-ideal outcomes. Rather than brushing those less-than-glossy experiences under the carpet, they are comfortable with sharing their full story – warts and all – knowing that countless others may be at a crossroads. They may be on the cusp of making the same questionable decisions, or they are already down the path and are looking for a way to backtrack and take the other route.

These authors are driven by purpose. Leaving anything out is a disservice to them and to the readers. I grew up in an era where, to be seen as successful, you had to have a shiny exterior and be perceived to live a flawless life. But when the gloss wore off and the truth began to be exposed, the ramifications of the ensuing fall from grace were catastrophic.

While there are still remnants of this former mask-like existence in society, I am so pleased that we live in an era where authenticity reigns. People are more cautious than ever of that which isn't what it seems and have become quite adept at sniffing out inauthentic representations. The remedy for this is simple – remain yourself and speak your truth.

Audience

'To write well, express yourself like the common people, but think like a wise man.'

Aristotle, Greek philosopher

'Oh, my book is for everyone!' is a common response from aspiring authors when I first chat with them about their ideal reader. While it is true that their story may hold elements that could interest or help people from all walks of life, writing your book while thinking the whole world is your audience only results in not reaching anyone in a meaningful way.

It's lovely to think that everyone could pick up a book and get what they need from it, but the danger for an author who comes at their project from that angle is running the risk of being too generic.

The first rule of any form of marketing is to have an ideal 'client' in mind. When it comes to writing a book, you switch this out for an ideal reader. Once again, it comes down to connection. You have connected to yourself through your 'why' and you have connected boldly to sharing your authentic story; now you need to connect all the above with your audience. This means getting clear on who your ideal reader is. You need to write for 'someone', not 'everyone'.

Not to worry... this won't discount every other person on the planet who doesn't fit your ideal reader mould. You may be familiar with the bell curve. It is widely used in the world of mathematics and is a graph that looks like an upside-down bell. It is used to illustrate a concept called normal distribution, which explains the probability of outcomes.

Why am I bringing this up in a book about writing? Well, when you look at who your ideal reader is, this is the person who fits all the criteria you are looking for in the person your book will have the most impact on. This person sits at the top of your bell curve. In statistical terms, this is 'the mode' by which all criteria are judged.[11]

Because the natural curve of the bell falls softly to either side until it reaches the bottom, you can see that as the person picking up the book varies slightly from your ideal reader characteristics, they will fall on either side of the dropping curve.

What this means is that although your book's ideal reader may be women who are in their thirties, divorced and with children, you may also attract women from other age brackets who are single or happily married and may be childless. These readers are not those you are writing for and marketing to, but they are attracted to your book for other reasons and will still be receptive to what it is you want to share.

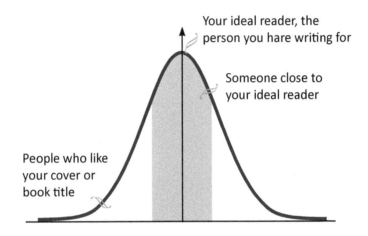

They may love your message, your book cover, or your title. They may even love you as a person and simply want to see what you have to say. The beauty of this is that while you may be aiming for a particular reader or market, surprise niches can pop up and give you a wider reach than expected.

> By writing for your ideal reader, you *are not* discounting these other readers by any means.

But what you *are* doing is being very clear on the way in which you write and present your story. Instead of writing to please everyone, you only need to please that someone. Believe me, it takes so much pressure off your writing process and makes it easier to determine what is relevant and what is not.

Zoë Sparks is an award-winning business powerhouse who has released a trilogy of books – *Strive & Thrive, Healthy & Wealthy* and *Award & Reward*. She has also collated another series called *SHINE'ing The Spotlight* which shares success stories of businesswomen. I was fortunate enough to feature in the first book of the series. With five books under her belt, you could say Zoë has well and truly caught the book bug! When sharing her writing journey on *The Phoenix Phenomenon*®, Zoë says she has always been clear on the audience she is catering for – businesswomen who are in the first few years of being self-employed.

'We started to get a bit of a reputation when the business, me personally, and my staff were winning awards and performing really well. People would gravitate towards me asking me to mentor them and help them on their own journeys. That's something that's always been a huge passion of mine. I'm very passionate about leadership, reward, recognition, and helping people to be the best they can be. As my business continued to grow, I started to not have so much time to give to other women who were setting themselves up in business. I was unable to spend quality time with them, helping them navigate through. I started to write down everything I'd learned personally. I thought, *If I can write these down as tips or advice and pull it together in some sort of document, I can send that out to people.* It was as if I would have a conversation with them through that platform. This document became my first self-published book. [The series] started out as my way of business coaching, and I'm not a professional business coach in any shape or form but I love to mentor, and this was a great way I could continue to share and help.'

It is important to define who your ideal reader is because the way in which you communicate to C-level executives is very different to how you would communicate to those who are still in their first years of business. The latter were Zoë's ideal readers. The language would be different for the two readers as would the examples and the way you structure your book.

I will give you a journalistic analogy because that's just my jam. The five *w's* and the *h* are questions that make up the core of any news story. Answering these questions ensures that you haven't left out any vital details. When it comes to identifying your ideal reader, these questions fit like a glove and provide you with clarity in uncovering the profile of this mystery 'someone'.

Your ideal reader

Schedule some time to really think about these key questions:

Who is your ideal reader? Who can you help?

- What is their age?
- What is their geographic location?
- What is their socioeconomic status?
- What is their career?
- Does gender or marital status matter?

What can you teach them?

- What are their problems?
- What do they want to know?
- What are their barriers to getting help or learning the message/lesson?
- What are the main lived experiences you've had?
- What are the amazing golden nuggets that you can share?

How did you come to possess this amazing information or story? (How did you learn your 'what'?)

- Book smarts?
- The school of life?
- Research?
- Receiving a diagnosis?

When do you want to connect with your reader?

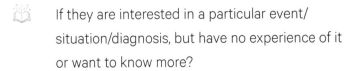 If they are interested in a particular event/situation/diagnosis, but have no experience of it or want to know more?

While they are in the midst of a particular event/situation/diagnosis and need help?

After they've overcome a particular event/situation/diagnosis and need help moving on?

In short, are they most likely to benefit from coming in at the beginning, middle, or end of your story?

Where do you want their mind to shift to by the time they finish reading your book?

What is the clear message you want them to take away?

Are there any clear actions they know they need to take based on what they have read?

Your *where* becomes important when you begin to write because it guides your messaging and the themes of the anecdotes you choose to share. If you have trouble deciding what this is, think about the best possible feedback you could get from a reader if they write to you and say, 'Your book changed my life because it taught me...' Really dig deep to think about what would give you a natural high or inspire a happy dance once you read it. Here's a hint – it may very well be connected to your 'why'.

Why is the fifth *w*, which we have already covered in the 'Self' section earlier in this chapter.

Once you have determined who your ideal reader is, you can keep them firmly in mind when structuring and planning the content for your book. Keep the responses to these questions handy as they will be invaluable when you reach Book Two, *The Structured Author*.

Here's something that may just blow your mind: nine times out of ten, I've found that your ideal reader is a past version of you! It was how you were thinking and feeling, or where you were, months, years, or even decades before you set out to write your book and share your story.

Fear of judgement

> *'It is hard to fail, but it is worse never to have tried to succeed.'*
>
> Theodore Roosevelt, conservationist, historian, and writer who served as the 26th president of the United States

I get it, it's tough opening up your heart and soul and putting it on display for all to read. It takes guts to even take the first step and commit to becoming an author. But as you are typing away, a little voice pipes up, *What will they think of me?* This thought alone is often enough to stop some aspiring authors in their tracks.

As Joshua Clifton said while a guest on *The Phoenix Phenomenon®*:

'It's just that old reptilian brain kicking in. It's just a safety mechanism. If we're not liked by a lot of people, there's that subconscious feeling that we might not fit in... isolation, death... all those things. We're going a bit deep here, but that's what it stems from. Realise that by writing this book you're going to be okay, you're going to survive. Yeah, you're going to get some naysayers, but then you're going to help a lot of people too. Is it worth the risk? Hell yeah. So, if you're coming from a place of truth, authenticity, and honesty, and know that your story will help others, it's always going to be the right decision to keep going.'

I wish I could say that no one will say a bad word about you or your future book, but that would make me a liar. Unfortunately, the way of the world is to judge, and the human condition means we are averse to being judged. Ironically, some of the content of your future book may centre on the fact you made some decisions or took some actions based on what others might think of you only for you to discover it was to your detriment.

Joshua's point cuts to the heart of the matter – there will always be people who won't like you, won't like your message, or won't like the way you deliver it. The key determinant between those who let the fear of judgement quash their authorship dreams and those who power through is one simple thing – the latter simply don't care what others think. They are so connected to their purpose for writing the book that the people who are going to criticise become a blur in the background, of little significance, and certainly not a gigantic hurdle they feel they need to leap over.

When Shari Hall was a guest on *The Phoenix Phenomenon®*, she shared how she had lost one of her longest friends after releasing her memoir *Perfect Love* in 2021. The subtitle of Shari's book is *One Woman's Journey From Flesh to Faith,* and it covers her evolution as a woman from the young girl who was driven by success and bodily pleasures through her journey of self-discovery, self-love and, ultimately, finding her true north in her faith. Shari did not shy away from sharing every detail of what her younger years entailed and this friend, who only knew her as Shari the successful anaesthetist and mother-of-two, could not accept that she had ever been anything different.

Of course, it was sad for Shari to lose this friend, but it only served to cement her resolve that people needed to experience her full journey to appreciate the magnitude of her evolution. She never wavered from her decision to bare all to the world because she knew there were other women out there who were still stuck in projecting a version of themselves that was inauthentic. She wanted to reach them and gently encourage them out of their cocoons so they could experience the freedom and joy of being who they are and embracing that woman – warts and all.

> If you find yourself worried what others will think of your book, revisit your 'why' and connect in with it.

How does it feel when you read your 'why' aloud? Do you feel empowered and driven to continue? Can you see the people you are going to help... your ideal reader? What do you imagine *they* will say to you? Counterbalance the negative with as much positive as you can and make this your focus.

When speaking to Erin Barnes, author of *The Whole Life Success Planner* and *My Best Life Planner – for kids,* the Next Generation Wellness founder shared how she was able to overcome her initial fear of judgement.

'I'll be the first to say my greatest fear is criticism. My belief is around anything that we do: if the necessity is not driving us, if there's not somebody else's need that is stronger – or our own – then we won't get anything done. If I just had the desire to release [the book] for me, it wouldn't have been enough. That sneaky voice would have come in every time, *Who do you think you are?* But the necessity was clear when I was speaking to people each day, thinking, *They don't have the funds to be able to invest in this. They need something to keep their head in the right spot and to feel like their life has purpose.* It was much easier to get out of my own way. I think it's a really nice thing for us all to remember that we all doubt, and so the moment we go to judge ourselves, we must pull back and remember nothing in the world would get created for us to enjoy if everyone felt the resistance to being judged and gave in.'

Once upon a time, self-publishing a book was seen as 'Vanity Press' and only used by people who were desperate to say they were an author without the backing of a traditional publisher. Today, the environment is very different and, with advances in technology, aspiring authors are empowered by having the choice between pursuing a traditional publisher for their work or going it alone and making their own mark on their own terms through self- or independently publishing. If those terms are new to you, do not despair as I will cover this in Book Three, *The Published Author*.

It's true there will always be literary purists who will turn their nose up at self-published authors, but the reality is that even a traditional publishing contract does not guarantee you will sell hundreds of thousands of books and become an international superstar. You *might*, but it all comes down to how you leverage it. With the onus falling back on the author to make their book a success, countless first-time authors are taking back control and doing things on their own terms with great success. Some of the bonuses of self- or indie publishing include a greater return on investment for each book sold, full ownership of your work and control over when, where, and how it is released.

But for some, it's hard not to feel the pull towards waiting for a traditional publisher to show interest in their work before they begin to seriously focus on writing their book. Leigh Robshaw was among them. I was fortunate enough to be working alongside Leigh as a journalist while she was writing her book in every spare waking moment she had between her work as a journalist and raising her two young boys. Leigh was driven to secure a publishing contract and even had several meetings with a high-profile Australian influencer who was preparing to launch her own publishing company, but nothing came to fruition. A couple of rejection letters from other publishers later, Leigh decided to bite the bullet and go for it herself, but she openly shared how she felt people would think she was 'up herself' for self-publishing her memoir.

> 'It was a gradual process of letting go of what anyone was going to think of me, and I believe any writer or artist will have to get to that point to be able to be true to their art form. With any art form, you're putting your soul out on a plate for the world to consume and either spit out or enjoy. Really, you've just got to do it and put it out there and then hope some people like it. My biggest fears were: *What if people say it's shit? What if people say I'm a bad writer or it's a boring story or I'm so up myself writing this story or whatever.* You're allowed to indulge your creativity and produce something that you feel proud of that you can share with the world. It doesn't mean you're egotistical or egocentric because you want to put a book out into the world.'

Leigh's lesson was based on letting go of the ego. No longer caring what the negative Nellies would think of her and instead being comfortable in supporting her own self-esteem. Ego is a word that is often misunderstood and often, it has quite negative connotations attached to it. For example, if someone has a big ego, they have a high opinion of themselves. In the case of becoming an author, many aspiring writers believe that the very act of publishing a book about themselves could lead to others thinking they have an enlarged ego. It is the ego that also leads us to judge ourselves and for others to feel entitled to judge us.

In *Think Like a Monk,* Jay Shetty writes, 'The ego is two-faced. One moment it tells us we're great at everything, and the next moment it tells us we're the worst. Either way, we are blind to the reality of who we are. True humility is seeing what lies between the extremes.'[12]

He gives some incredible contrasts between the inflated ego versus having a healthy self-esteem which I think are incredibly important for aspiring authors grappling with a fear of judgement to understand.

'Ego fears what people will say; self-esteem filters what people say.

Ego compares to others; self-esteem compares to themselves.

Ego wants to prove themselves; self-esteem wants to be themselves.

Ego knows everything; self-esteem can learn from anyone.

Ego pretends to be strong; self-esteem is okay being vulnerable.

Ego wants people to respect them; self-esteem respects self and others.'

If you find you continue to feel like you are looking for external validation and worrying about what others think of you and your future book, take time to revisit your 'why' and understand the uniqueness that makes you the best person to serve them.

Come back to that connection to self. Until you realise how amazing you are, others won't be able to see you truly shine.

I don't want to upset people I know

'Life is just too damn short to let someone else's opinion steer the wheel.'

Dave Grohl, Foo Fighters frontman
and author of *The Storyteller*

If you are writing about your life experiences, chances are there will be other characters who are integral to telling your story and they may not always be heroes and heroines. It is a common concern for many who write a memoir or autobiographical piece to worry about upsetting people in the process, even though you *really* want to write your book and speak your truth.

There is a quote I love which states, 'When your passion and purpose are greater than your fears and excuses, you will find a way.' If you fear that your ex-girlfriend from Year 6 will read your book and get a little bit ticked off, it is an easy decision to choose to be courageous and write about it.

However, the delicate dance between fear and purpose can become more complicated when the people you may affect include members of your family or close friends. The ballgame is elevated to a whole new level as there is much more at stake. The equation of passion and purpose versus fears and excuses still comes into play here and you've got to weigh it up. Could you potentially save lives by sharing your lived experience? How would that compare to potentially upsetting people who love you? How would you feel if you allowed your life's purpose to help others to fade because your family might not know the intimate details of your life you are about to share?

We can spend much longer than necessary *assuming* we know how other people are going to feel about the things we have to say.

All this does is create extra stress in your life and that is something you could do without.

The go-to solution in this case is to approach the people in question and request their permission for you to include them in your book. I appreciate that when you are dealing with people close to you and writing about events that could be traumatic or less than glossy, these are difficult conversations to have. But having their nod of approval (you may want to get it in writing depending on the circumstances) will set you free.

Ways to address concerns from people appearing in your book

For people with whom you do have a relationship, this can be fixed through a simple conversation. *Ask* them how they would feel if you mentioned situations that may involve them.

Remember to tell them:

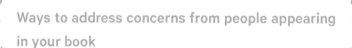 This book is about me and my thoughts/feelings/experiences and will be worded as such.

I am not setting out to make you look good or to paint you in a bad light; I simply want to share my truth.

I believe sharing the situation could really help people.

Once you have asked the question, you can get a clear indication of where they stand. This doesn't need to be heavy – you can show them the relevant chapters and ask for their approval. If they genuinely don't want to be identified, make it a game to see who can come up with the most creative fake name for them.

If a brick wall of resistance remains, you have two options.

The first is to reassess how important their role is to your story. If the person in question can be removed without leaving a gaping hole and this relationship is important to you, you may consider replacing it with another, more relevant story. However, if it is pivotal, you do have the final say over whether it is printed, even if it may compromise the relationship. Yes, it is tricky territory but only you can navigate it.

Two options: keep the story or cut it

When the people you may upset are no longer active in your life or have been estranged for some time and you have no desire to reach out to them, talking it through may not be an option.

If there is someone who you have no desire to reach out to or be in contact with and you want to keep their stories, there are some rules that should not be broken:

 Avoid the blame game at all costs. Finger-pointing, justification, and blame will not serve you in any way, shape, or form. It is petty and your readers will disconnect if they sense that you are not prepared to own your own actions.

We all have those moments in our lives when we could have chosen a better path. Shirking responsibilities for poor choices made will not only rub your readers the wrong way, but it is also a sure-fire way to upset the people you are painting as the 'villains'.

 Don't get me wrong, there absolutely are villains in life. People who commit criminal acts should never be fluffed over or their actions diminished, especially in stories that deal with domestic or sexual violence, however you can avoid opening a can of litigious worms by staying within your own lane. Share events and situations firmly from your point of view and stick to facts.

 Don't attempt to put the reader into the mind of another person, because you can never truly *know* what they were thinking or feeling. You can only give your best guess and that is where your book risks becoming a potential libel or slander case. By writing how you perceived the events to have unfolded, describing how it made you feel and the lessons you took away from it, you reduce the potential for people to take you to task. Just as you can't articulate what someone else is thinking or feeling, they can't do the same to you.

If an event has been documented in the media or in court and there is a public record of it, you can absolutely use these *facts* in your book. If you do this without embellishing and twisting things to make them more dramatic, the person or people in question will rarely get very far in pursuing any legal action against you.

 Don't be tempted to play with the truth so either you or others can save face. If you are presenting a non-fiction book, you need to remain true to the facts.

 It probably goes without saying, but publishing any confidential or classified information will only get you into trouble.

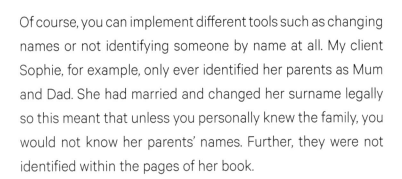

Of course, you can implement different tools such as changing names or not identifying someone by name at all. My client Sophie, for example, only ever identified her parents as Mum and Dad. She had married and changed her surname legally so this meant that unless you personally knew the family, you would not know her parents' names. Further, they were not identified within the pages of her book.

I want to be clear, though, that changing names doesn't give you a free pass to write whatever you want without consequence.

If you realise the event linked with a person is not integral to the themes and the overall message, you can cut it from the manuscript completely.

There is, of course, the potential for things to swing much more heavily into the positive. You may reach out to ask the question and find that a relationship is repaired. Or when they finally read your story, they may see you through new eyes with a whole new perspective of you after learning what you have endured in life.

When chatting to Leon Stensholm, author of *It's How You Think*, on *The Phoenix Phenomenon*®, he said it was his mother who had the most surprised reaction when she read his book, which covered the loss of his brother and close friends to suicide and his own failed suicide attempt when he became overwhelmed with grief.

> 'I think Mum rang me straight away and she goes, "How could you feel that way? You're always happy. I wouldn't imagine you could feel that way." I said, "Mum, well, like I guess that's lesson number one, isn't it? You never really know what someone's going through." There would have been times when she asked me how I was and, like the next person, I'm going to say I'm fantastic. But it wasn't hard to understand that I wasn't fantastic. I was tired, I hadn't slept. I was a little bit moody, a little bit short with people. This taught me that

no one around me had any physiology identification skills of individuals, so I need to teach people that now.'

Remember, when you write strictly from your point of view and don't give thoughts or dialogue to a third-party character that assume what they would think or feel, you will be giving yourself the best possible protection against legal recourse.

Upsetting people is not a legal issue, but defamation is.

Navigating defamation

Defamation is one of the most common legal issues authors could encounter – the second is breach of copyright, which you can avoid by thoroughly referencing any quotes, research, and song lyrics you may use. The definition of defamation is 'the act of damaging the good reputation of someone'.

A defamation claim can be made by someone if:

- the material is not supported by facts.
- the person or business was clearly identified.
- the material caused or is continuing to cause 'serious harm' to their reputation.[13]

To use extreme examples, you wouldn't call someone a paedophile or a murderer in your book unless they had been judicially tried and convicted of such offences. Court documents are 'facts' and in the public domain so therefore will provide protection against claims of defamation. In high-stakes cases like this, you would not rely on obscuring the identity of someone in order to feel safe to throw accusations around. Unless the person you are writing about was actually convicted of committing the crimes, don't go there.

The way defamation laws are structured varies in each country and even in states within countries, so I recommend you seek advice from a lawyer if you have major concerns. It is always better to err on the side of caution, and while it may be an undesirable expense upfront, it can pay off if a consultation with a lawyer saves you from addressing concerns notices (the initial stages of a defamation suit) or litigation.

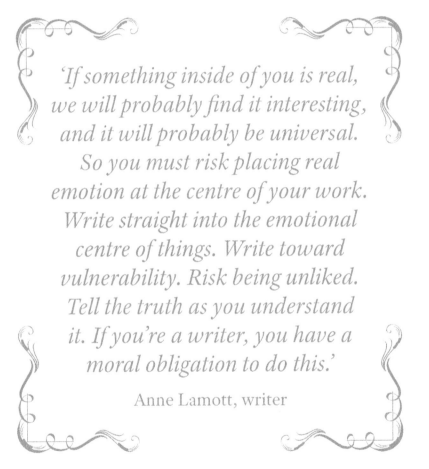

'If something inside of you is real,
we will probably find it interesting,
and it will probably be universal.
So you must risk placing real
emotion at the centre of your work.
Write straight into the emotional
centre of things. Write toward
vulnerability. Risk being unliked.
Tell the truth as you understand
it. If you're a writer, you have a
moral obligation to do this.'

Anne Lamott, writer

Transformation

Becoming an author is about so much more than simply slapping words between two covers – it's about the journey and the **transformation**.

Let me be the first to tell you that standing up and owning your story is a true sign of *bravery*.

Yes, you could choose to focus solely on the surface and still have a good book, but if you are aiming for a *game-changing* book for you, your business, and your future readers, you must be open to the possibility of transformation.

When I talk about transformation, I mean becoming more comfortable in your own skin, unapologetically owning your past and present, creating absolute certainty about the purpose and focus of your business and who you can help and, most importantly, how people can learn real lessons and become inspired by your book.

The ripple effect then reaches the readers and they in turn are transformed. For your readers, their transformation begins when they pick up your book and read the content you have crafted for them. They will resonate with the content and then apply it to their own lives. When they relate to you and your journey, they will be more inclined to learn from your mistakes and make changes to their lives that could switch their trajectory towards an imminently better future. All because of you!

That cycle of empowerment of your sharing, their understanding then enacting positive change is one that has the potential to carry on for as long as you allow it. How is that not transformational?

> Authors are some of the bravest people around – they are prepared to stand behind their message, accept their mistakes, and showcase them in a bid to help others.

The power of transformation

In my time as a ghostwriter and writing mentor, I have seen unique transformations for every single one of the authors I have worked with.

They have been as varied as:

 healing past traumas

 coming to terms with how their life has evolved

 re-establishing relationships they thought they had lost

 stepping into their power now that they completely own their message

- creating new and exciting opportunities such as hosting and appearing on podcasts and being invited to speak on stage
- becoming selfless in their quest to help others
- being able to charge more for their services
- becoming recognised as an expert in their field.

Country music sensation and author of *Backstage Nashville*, Wayne Warner, who is no stranger to success and achievement, says becoming an author helped him to 'enjoy my nows'.

'When writing, I was going through all these great things that I had lived through, but I realised I had not really appreciated them. We were on tour and released a hit record. I became a father. I worked with Taylor Swift and with all these renowned artists, and I was all very blasé about it. I've really learned to enjoy my nows now because I didn't enjoy my nows then. I think in the process of writing this book, I really regretted that. I wasn't present before.'

Leon Stensholm, author of *It's How You Think*, also shared his transformation with viewers of *The Phoenix Phenomenon*® and said writing his book was 'probably the only time I'd ever done therapy'.

'I had all this stuff in my mind and once I put it on paper, it brought up good memories and triumphs as well as old wounds. It brought up things that I'd actually forgotten about.'

The same happened for Barry Bull, a multi-international bestselling author, when he wrote his latest title, *UnbreakaBULL*. Barry sought my help in early 2019 because this book was very different to the rest of his catalogue. He had become renowned as a music industry icon and savvy businessman and his straightforward books were anchored in the how-to realm. He started writing *UnbreakaBULL* as narrative therapy after losing his beloved wife of fifty-two years.

This book was the most personal he had ever been and lifted the veil between his widely known business persona and the devoted husband. Barry said writing this book allowed him to process his grief and come back to himself. In the throes of loss, he couldn't bear to pick up his guitar and play. He said it was like the music had 'gone out of him'. A changed and very energised Barry fronted a sell-out crowd at the Mooloolaba Surf Club in early 2021 when he released his book and entertained the crowd with some of the songs that were pivotal to his love story. It was amazing to play even a small role in that type of transformation.

I have had the privilege of interviewing internationally renowned children's author Andy Griffiths following the release of his latest book, *143-Storey Treehouse*, which was illustrated by his long-time creative partner Terry Denton.

I am always curious about the transformations people go through when they become authors. With Andy being a former school teacher, I wanted to know what the bridge between the classroom and authorship looked like for Andy, so I asked him the same question I've asked everyone who has appeared on *The Phoenix Phenomenon®* series: 'What do you think your greatest transformation has been?'

His answer – as they always are – was powerful:

'I think for me, suddenly everything made sense. My whole life made sense, my love of nonsense, love of humour, my love of reading, messing around and laughing at things that had no real point. Suddenly it all kind of gelled and I thought, *Oh my God, I can do something useful with this!* In my late twenties, early thirties, I first encountered students in my class who hated reading. I knew I needed to turn them around on this. At first, I thought I'd have to try to be a professional and get serious. That never felt good or natural. I was putting it on. I did notice anything I told that had a humorous angle was always well received. I thought, *Maybe I'm a humour writer?* When I gave the kids little books I had written myself to get them engaged with reading, they were a hit. It was all obvious in retrospect but to me, at the time, that was a revelation. I knew I had to pursue this humour and didn't care if anybody else got it. A lot of my heroes are outsider artists who do their own thing and the audience comes to them. It was a bold decision at the time because I was clearly not a John Marsden or Paul Jennings. But when Terry appeared, it was this life-affirming thing. He picked up on the frequency that I was transmitting on, and the kids did too. They get it immediately and don't need it explained to them. The key to happiness is having access to all parts of your personality. Childhood awakens us to imagination and fun. It provides pleasure of the present moment without worrying about what it's all leading to or what happened yesterday. Take pleasure in this very moment... there is an enormous amount of pleasure to be had if you allow yourself to just have fun.'

Imagine the type of transformation that awaits you?

Those who can align their book with their business or professional goals have the potential to unlock new opportunities or even lift their price ceiling to attract high-end clients. This is because being an author of a high-quality book is still held in high esteem in professional circles. You are elevated to expert status and with some great marketing behind you, the potential to leverage your book to become an industry commentator, a renowned leader, a sought-after consultant, and even a speaker on a global scale is limitless – you can take it as far as you want to.

One of my gold-star clients in terms of leveraging a book for business is Stew Darling. I was a ghostwriter for Stew, and I can share his name because Stew is one of the few clients I have ghosted for who has been very open and shared this publicly, which I am grateful for.

Stew came to me in 2019 because he had developed a framework to be able to coach people on how to tap into their inner leader. He called it Lead through Life. Fortuitously, this also became the name of his book. Stew wanted to create a book that would step people through the framework in a very clear how-to style akin to some of his favourite mentors such as Brendon Burchard.

His framework was sound and had a very clear progression of building upon different skillsets to reach the goal of well-rounded leader. But I knew there was much more to Stew than just his intellectual property.

Stew was a former British Army officer with a career that spanned from just after his eighteenth birthday until he took command of all UK military intelligence training, responsible for leadership and professional training for over 10,000 students. In between, he served in the Middle East and was a covert operative and undertook some awesome James Bond-esque spy jobs!

To ignore all of that would have meant he was only sharing half of himself – the professional self – while the personal self who had experienced all these amazing, shocking, and awe-inspiring things was left out in the cold. Interestingly, it was the personal self who had learned all the lessons that allowed the professional self to develop such an incredible leadership framework.

> Isn't it funny how professionals tend to separate their work self from their personal self?

I was guilty of doing just that when I first started out in business. I was too worried my laid-back, slightly goofy self was too unpolished to be seen as professional. I've well and truly proven that wrong by embracing my goofy self and sharing my passion and being rewarded with business awards.

It's time to realise the power of amalgamating the professional and the personal, a motto I spruiked constantly during my Leverage Your Story sessions in libraries across the Sunshine Coast at the end of 2021. When you put yourself forward as a whole person, your ability to connect with your readers skyrockets!

Stew quickly saw this would be the best way forward for his book, so we were able to integrate both his lived experience and his learned knowledge to create a book that has been changing lives since it was released in early 2020.

He has leveraged *Lead through Life* to the hilt since then! Stew is now renowned as New Zealand's top resilience coach, hosting sell-out seminars across the country to help thousands while also building his own business empire. He has developed new programs and brought his wife into the business to expand the offerings after he discovered a niche in upskilling parents, who are the overseers of the next generation of leaders. Stew also hosts a weekly radio segment called *The Resilient Show*.

All the above has meant he has well and truly placed himself in the expert realm and is being widely recognised for that by the mainstream media. Whenever there is something that requires commentary around leadership, Kiwi radio, television and newspapers reach out to Stew for comment. He no longer needs to send out press releases in the hope he will get a run and have his message out there – the media are coming to him!

All of this was possible with a book as his launchpad. All of this is also possible for you if you have the determination to see it through!

There is a lingering train of thought out there that there is mega money to be made from selling books. Unless you are one of the fortunate who manages to reach international bestseller and sell tens of thousands of books, that is unlikely. However, you *can* channel your inner Stew and leverage your book to create pillars off which you can build just about anything for you or your business. It is in selling those products or services that you can really make your book work for you and generate far more income than the $29.99 cover price.

To be fully transparent, this book is absolutely a pillar for me. I created it to serve people like you who want to have the tools you need to be able to write the book you have always dreamed of. It is the logical stepping-off point for people who do not yet know me or trust that I have the knowledge and experience to get them there.

However, the next step is not so clearly defined and depends purely on what fits you best. You may be able to follow this guide and the rest of the trilogy and realise your dream without any more help from me. That would be amazing!

You may realise you do need more guidance and because we have developed a rapport through the pages of this book, you will feel more comfortable reaching out for help and may sign up for my in-person or online *Ignite & Write* small group coaching days.

This leads into my twelve-week *Ignite & Write* mentorship for those who want to feel supported throughout their writing journey.

You may decide to skip writing altogether and engage me to be your ghostwriter. This is not something to be ashamed of. You can save yourself a whole lot of time, energy, and heartache if you know that writing is not your strength or something you wish to get better at. In fact, it can be the most liberating thing to unburden yourself and still come out the other end with the same amazing book you had wanted to create – minus the headaches!

So now it's your turn – if you were to have a blue-sky vision for what was possible for you, what pillars would you like to build around your future book?

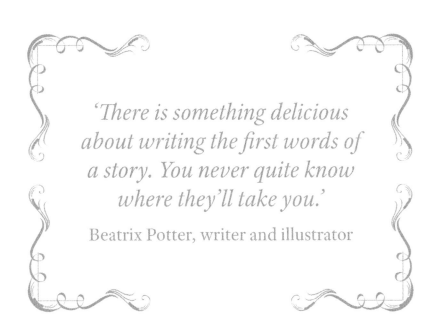

'There is something delicious
about writing the first words of
a story. You never quite know
where they'll take you.'

Beatrix Potter, writer and illustrator

The pep talk

D id you know that you can destroy your own chance of embarking on the journey of writing the first words of your book? I was contacted by a lady – let's call her Maddi – who had completed a degree in creative writing. Maddi wanted me to be her ghostwriter. Not because she didn't have the time or the skills but because she doubted her own ability.

I encouraged Maddi to let me mentor her through the process so she could put that hard-earned degree to good use, but she would not budge. She was so firmly stuck in her 'I'm not a good writer' mindset that she could not see any other way to complete her book. Her story was unique in that she had survived a rare cancer so I obliged, and we worked together to unleash her story.

If you find your mindset remains firmly stuck in 'don't know how' or any of the other common hurdles for first-time authors, you can always rely on this book to give you everything you need to clear those how-to challenges with ease and head straight for the finish line where your own book can be out there, serving the world.

So now you have a choice; you can continue to allow your mindset to be the ball and chain that anchors you to the start line, keeping you completely out of the race, or you can act and find the wind under your wings that propels you forward and sees you finish ahead of the pack with a book you know will change lives.

You've got *The Phoenix Phenomenon®* ACT process so you can ignite your passion and write your book.

Imagine your book becoming the very thing someone *needs* to inspire positive action in their own lives. Imagine being able to provide it for them and becoming the beacon or the turning point in their life.

It is all possible.

It is all within you.

All you need to do is to ACT.

So, what is the next step? If you are feeling confident continuing your journey at your own pace at home, get hold of the remainder of the *Ignite & Write* trilogy.

Book Two in this series – *The Structured Author* – will take the guesswork out of how to write your book! You will be able to draw all the thoughts, ideas, and memories out of your mind and create a structure that contains every important element to keep your reader enthralled from start to end.

The Structured Author is also jam-packed full of information that will help you determine what style of book best suits your story and how to structure everything from the overall manuscript right down to the anatomy of a captivating chapter so you can write with passion and purpose. You can get your copy at www.roxannewriter.com.

If you feel like you need assistance with that next step, I am here for you! My *Ignite & Write* small group coaching days are held regularly throughout the year both in person and online, so you can dial in from anywhere in the world in your pyjamas if you wish and get everything you need.

Just as Book Two does, the *Ignite & Write* coaching days help you bust through mindset hurdles and guide you through the foundational steps required to build an engaging chapter outline for a book that has the power to transform you, your business, and the lives of your future readers. This day is for you if you already have a non-fiction book idea and you have the dedication and passion that requires some guidance and knowledge to steer you in the right direction.

By joining the intimate *Ignite & Write* small group coaching day, you will delve deeper into *The Phoenix Phenomenon*® ACT process, which provides clear and easy steps to build strong foundations for your book manuscript. You will become aware of the inner self-talk that can hold you back from writing your book and become more empowered than ever before to reach your goal. You will also feel more connected to yourself, your story, and your audience, which will propel you through any future hurdles to becoming the author you've always dreamed of.

You will have greater clarity of your purpose for writing a book, know how meaningful it is to share it with the world and be at peace with your past and your present so you are ready to launch into a great future. All of this will be achieved in a focused setting among like-minded people over a day of connection.

Just like you, I also had a choice when it came to methods of educating aspiring authors.

I could throw open the doors to every aspiring author and host day seminars where I could fill the room and share my knowledge with everyone. This means I could reach more people for sure, however, if I opened these seminars to such a broad audience, I would also have to keep my content on a very generic level.

Or I could keep these groups intimate so I could get to know every one of the authors and their stories and give them personalised guidance. This more intimate approach allows you to walk away with a narrative structure in place for *your* story so you can start writing right away! There won't be a single generic template in sight.

When I looked at my options like that, my decision to keep it intimate was a no-brainer.

The atmosphere at my 2019, 2021 and 2022 workshops (yes, there was a gap for Covid-19!) has been electric and it has been heartwarming to attend book launches for people who have attended and gone on to fulfil their dream of becoming authors!

One such person is Shari Hall, the author of *Perfect Love*.

'What a privilege to have the opportunity to work with Roxanne. Around the time I began writing my memoir, I attended one of her book writing workshops. Little did I know that experience would lead to the development of a wonderful relationship. Roxanne has mentored, suggested, read, and reviewed my 640-page book and, every step of the way, her guidance has been invaluable – from suggested edits and comments to format and structure. And when it was all finished, she went above and beyond ensuring I was connected to all the right people to move my project forward. I highly recommend working with this astounding woman.'

Another was De Paole, whom I had a one-on-one planning session with.

'It has been incredibly therapeutic to be able to finally figure out what happened to me from birth. For the first time in my life, I am slowly finding my voice. I have you to thank for getting me going.'

If you have read this book and decided writing is not the path for you, do not despair! My passion is writing, and I would be honoured to connect with you to talk through your book vision and discuss how I can assist as your ghostwriter.

As your ghostwriter, I will work alongside you to get to know your story intimately and we will create your manuscript outline together. I will then deploy my interviewing skills, honed since 2007, to gather the content I need to then write your book. Your time investment is minimal – just the planning and interview sessions. The rest of the work is up to me!

I take your words and create magic, weaving it all together into a manuscript that will take your reader on a journey and provide you with something you will be so proud of, you won't be able to wait to stand tall and share your authentic message with the world.

Authentic voice means everything to me, and if I can have the wife of a Vietnam veteran call me up after reading her husband's book draft to tell me she could hear his voice in her head as she read, chances are I can find your voice too!

You can find out more about my ghostwriting services or connect with me to find out at www.roxannewriter.com.

No matter which path you take, I wish you every success with fulfilling this dream of yours. Just remember, every small step you take forward will lead to your ultimate destination.

Happy writing!

Roxanne McCarty-O'Kane

Acknowledgements

Something as magical as a book rarely happens under the steam of a single person. While I may have written the words on these pages, they have been shaped and inspired by the many amazing people in my life, only some of whom I will be able to acknowledge here by name.

So, firstly, thank you to every single one of you who have touched my life in some way, either through friendship, connection through business, or being lumped with me as part of the family tree. You know who you are. Every single one of you has made an impact in my life for which I am grateful.

Special mention to my long-suffering husband, Chris, who has been my number one fan and supporter long before I had the courage to believe in myself. I could never have the strength to push myself further each year without knowing you have my back, always.

My cheebies, Lilly and Lincoln, who are every bit as crazy, creative, and wild as me. You have been my biggest teachers in life, and I love you both dearly. Your welcome distractions and open invitations to be a kid again have kept me connected to the inner child that creativity thrives off. Love you to the moon and back times infinity.

To Andy Kippen, who opened the door to the career that has shaped me. Thank you for giving this wide-eyed young'un a chance all those years ago.

Genine Howard, without you I would not have even thought that stepping away from the seven-to-eight of traditional media was a possibility for me. Carren Smith, my coach extraordinaire, thank you for continuing to open my eyes to the wonderful world of business and all that we can create if we remain open to the possibilities.

Mona de Vestel, thank you for being the perfectionist in this creative process and polishing up my pearls of wisdom until they shine with even more clarity than I could conjure up in my first draft. Your incredible feedback and creative suggestions have made this book everything I'd hoped it would be. You are a legend of your craft, and I am grateful to have you on my team.

Also a shout out to dear Candice Holznagel. We're lifers for sure, but your unwavering support and friendship is something I treasure. I can always count on you for constructive feedback and it was a necessity for this project. Thank you as always for your time and love.

Illustrator genius Cara Ord, you took my very abstract concept and idea for my phoenix image and created something so on point that I wanted three – one for each of the books in the trilogy. Your ability to craft emotive and meaningful graphics has been incredible to watch.

Thank you to Alex Fullerton and the team at Author Support Services. You have created this work of beauty that I am so incredibly proud of. Your guidance and support throughout the publishing journey have been priceless.

Last, but most definitely not least, thank you to *you* for trusting me to be your partner in this incredible, powerful, and uplifting journey that is authorship. I wish you every success and look forward to being among your growing number of cheerleaders. Stand tall, own your message, and make the difference you have always dreamed of.

About Roxy

Roxanne McCarty-O'Kane is a ghostwriter and writing mentor who works closely with aspiring authors to empower them to stand up and become the changemakers they dream to be through authorship.

Storytelling has been Roxanne's bread and butter since 2007 with a long career as a journalist for newspapers, magazines, and online publications before transferring her skillsets into non-fiction book creation.

Her emphasis on connection to her authors and honouring the uniqueness of their stories has seen her recognised in:

2021

 WINNER Micro/Small Business Woman in the Sunshine Coast Business Women's Network Awards.

 Australian Small Business Champion Awards Sole Trader Finalist.

2020

-  Australian Small Business Champion Awards Sole Trader Finalist.
- Australian My Business Awards for Young Leader of the Year Finalist (one of only two female finalists).
- 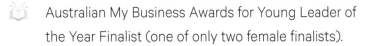 Australian My Business Awards for B2C Business of the Year Finalist.

2019

- Young Business Woman of the Year Finalist in the Sunshine Coast Business Women's Network Awards.
-  Australian My Business Awards Young Leader of the Year Finalist.

In 2021, Roxanne was recognised as an ambassador for no more fake smiles, a charity that provides advocacy and therapy for victims of child sexual abuse and their families.

When she isn't in her writing cave, leading *Ignite & Write* workshops, or mentoring aspiring authors, Roxanne enjoys asserting her dominance in family games of Bananagrams, playing her guitar, and ·curling up in the hammock on the back deck with a good book.

If you have been inspired by this book to pursue your dreams of becoming an author and want to work with Roxanne, connect with her on:

Instagram: @roxannewriter

Facebook: facebook.com/roxannewriter

LinkedIn: linkedin.com/in/roxannemccartyokane/

Website: www.roxannewriter.com

To watch any episodes of *The Phoenix Phenomenon*® mentioned in this book, visit www.roxannewriter.com.au/vlog/

References

1. William Dietrich, *The Writer's Odds of Success*. Huff Post, May 4, 2013. Retrieved on April 4, 2021, https://www. huffpost.com/entry/the-writers-odds-of-succe_b_2806611

2. Mal Warwick, *Would You Believe How Many Books Are Published Every Year in the U.S.?* Mal Warwick on Books, 2021. Retrieved on March 3, 2021, https:// malwarwickonbooks.com/published-every-year/

3. United States Census Bureau, www.census.gov

4. Steven Piersanti, *The 10 Awful Truths About Book Publishing*. Berrett-Koehler Publishers, June 24, 2020. Retrieved on May 16, 2021, https://ideas.bkconnection. com/10-awful-truths-about-publishing

5. Australian Bureau of Statistics (ABS), *Population*. Australian Bureau of Statistics, December 16, 2021. Retrieved on January 23, 2022, https://www.abs.gov.au/ statistics/people/population

6. Books+Publishing, *Publishing and the pandemic: The Australian book market in 2020*. Books+Publishing, September 30, 2020. Retrieved on January 23, 2022. https://www.booksandpublishing.com.au/

articles/2020/09/30/157402/publishing-and-the-pandemic-the-australian-book-market-in-2020/

7. Simon Sinek, *Start with Why: How Great Leaders Inspire Everyone to Take Action*. Portfolio, 2019.

8. Olivier Serrat, *Knowledge Solutions: The Five Whys Technique*. Chicago School of Professional Psychology, 2017. Retrieved on April 3, 2021, https://www.researchgate.net/publication/318013490_The_Five_Whys_Technique

9. Dr Sahar Yousef, *How to find your most creative time of day, and make it count*, It's Nice That, March 9, 2020. Retrieved on January 30, 2022, https://www.itsnicethat.com/news/sahar-yousef-most-creative-time-of-day-opinion-090320

10. Melissa Breyer, *8 Famous Authors Who Used Secret Pseudonyms*. ThoughtCo, May 17, 2020. Retrieved on December 23, 2021, https://www.thoughtco.com/famous-authors-who-used-secret-pseudonyms-4864216

11. Deb Russell, *Bell Curve and Normal Distribution Definition*. ThoughtCo, September 3, 2019. Retrieved on December 15, 2021, https://www.thoughtco.com/bell-curve-normal-distribution-defined-2312350

12. Jay Shetty, *Think Like a Monk: The secret of how to harness the power of positivity and be happy now*. HarperCollins UK, 2020.

13. Crown Law, *2021 Changes to Queensland defamation law*. Crown Law, August 5, 2021. Retrieved on March 29, 2022, https://www.crownlaw.qld.gov.au/resources/publications/2021-changes-to-queensland-defamation-law#:~:text=One%20of%20the%2

The _Ignite_ & _Write_ series

The Structured Author

Book Two in this series will take the guesswork out of _how_ to write your book! You will be guided through how to draw all the thoughts, ideas, and memories out of your mind and create a structure that contains every important element to keep your reader enthralled from start to end. It is also jam-packed full of information that will help you determine what style of book best suits your story and how to structure everything from the overall manuscript right down to the anatomy of a captivating chapter so you can write with passion and purpose.

The Published Author

Book Three is dedicated to what comes *after* you have finished that first draft. Discover the pros and cons of the different forms of publishing available to aspiring authors today and learn how to determine the best route for your book vision. Marketing is a vital, yet often overlooked, part of the process of becoming an author and this book reveals tips and tricks to set you on the right path.

To experience the full *Ignite & Write* journey, complete the trilogy and head to www.roxannewriter.com

CPSIA information can be obtained
at www.ICGtesting.com
Printed in the USA
LVHW072332280722
724664LV00019B/399